A Tithe of Time

WILLIAM JORDAN

ISBN: 098849891X
ISBN-13: 978-0988498914

DEDICATION

This book is dedicated to the man and woman who have had the greatest spiritual impact on my life:

to my grandmother, Carolyn Jordan, who made sure from an early age that I grew up in the church and had the opportunity to hear God's Word and to know God's love for me

and

to my dear friend Scott Meacham, who has been used by the Lord to bless countless lives and who taught me to love the Lord first of all and to look for God's will in all things in my life.

I dedicate this book to you both, that you may share in whatever fruit God brings though it, and that you may know the significant and eternal difference you have both made in my life.

.

CONTENTS

ACKNOWLEDGMENTS

This book and study was made possible with the feedback and support of many people in various ways.

I would specifically like to thank Pastor Dave Archuletta, Steve Corum and Scott Meacham for their reviews, edits, and suggestions for improving the book. I would also like to thank Pastor Phil Munsey, Pastor Dave Burns, and Josh McDowell for their support and encouragement.

In addition, I would like to acknowledge and thank Kristina Seleshanko for her editing and coaching on my writing and Annie Lima for editing of the book as well as completely handling the formatting and pre-publication process for both the electronic and print versions.

A final thanks to the many people who have encouraged the publication of *A Tithe of Time*.

Preface

The first question that goes through the minds of readers when they contemplate reading a particular book is usually something along the lines of, *Who is this author, and why did he feel compelled to write this book?* To answer these questions, let me begin by stating that I am not a pastor, I don't have a degree from a Christian university, and I've never spent a day in seminary. Even though I became a Christian at the age of eight, it really wasn't until I met my future bride that I began to truly develop a relationship with Christ.

However, I was called to write this book. God has been prompting me to do so for years, and I've delayed and stalled more than I should have. In December of 2006, my pastor challenged the congregation in several sermons at the end of the year. Among other things, he encouraged us to "finish that book."

At that time God had been telling me for almost two years to write this book and I'd done nothing. Those sermons motivated me to get to work. It took far longer than I expected, but this book is the result of a normal person, someone just like you, simply listening to God's voice and attempting to do what He has told me to do.

The purpose of this book is to help you have the relationship with the Lord that He wants you to have, and specifically to help you carve out time in your life to make room for that treasured relationship. It is my fervent desire that you will learn to better hear His voice and to find within your soul that great work that God has purposed for you to do. If you will give God the time He yearns to spend with you, I guarantee that you will hear His voice and draw closer to Him as a result.

Preface

Introduction

Christians today tend to be too busy and too stressed. We have lost the patience to "be still and know that (He is) God" (Psalm 46:10). The result of our busy, stressful way of life is that most Christians struggle to hear the "still small voice" of the Lord.

We are desperate to know God's will and purpose for our life, and we complain that God doesn't speak to us; yet we Christians often give God a little time on Sunday and not much else.

This book will challenge you to give God the time He desires, and it will do so by taking a unique approach: you will set aside the distractions of life for forty days to see what God will do when He becomes the focus of your attention.

When we give God a tithe of our resources, He tells us it is the same as if we had given it all to Him. The Lord even challenges us to give to Him. Can God do more for us with the 90% left after we tithe 10% than we can do for ourselves with 100% of our resources? Of course He can!

Therefore, if we pause to give our Lord a tithe of our time, He can do more with our lives in the remaining 90% than we have been able to do with all 100%. Of course He can!

Find God's plan for your life here on earth. Give Him the opportunity to show you the great work He has placed in your soul to accomplish for His glory. Experience the joy and peace of walking more closely with Him.

God has called you, and He has a definite plan for your life. He desires a more intimate relationship with you and is waiting for you to draw near to Him.

Since you have invested so much time in relationships with those here on earth, shouldn't you likewise invest time in your relationship with our Lord and Savior? God will bless you in this journey!

William Jordan

One
What's Wrong with How we Spend our Time?

You may have been drawn to pick up this book because something in you knows that you need to give the Lord a tithe of your time, yet at the same time you're probably thinking, *I don't have time to read this book!*

Yes, it is true -- reading this book will take time, and more than that, it will challenge you to reassess your priorities. It will take your focus off of consumption and gratification for a time, and it will help you sharpen your eternal perspective. It will change the way you manage your life, and yes, it will change the way you spend your time.

It seems that no one has time for anything anymore, least of all to read a book about how we spend our time!

However, if you will set aside forty days to read this book, I'll make you a promise: Your life will never be the same, and you will look back and decide this was one of the most positively life-changing books you have ever read!

You probably picked up this book because when you stop and think about it, you know that the life you are living is not the life you were destined to live. You sense that you can do so much more, be so much more, and yet you are falling short of your potential. Somewhere deep in your soul you know this, though you may not be able to explain how or why you know it.

If you take the time to read this book and follow the steps we will discuss, you will never regret it. When you are finished reading this book and following its study guide, you may well look back at this process as being the lever God used to transform your life into what He had always planned for it to be.

Now you are thinking, *Yes, I know -- that sounds like something I need, but I really don't have time to read another book!*

We are busier than ever before. If you are like me and billions of other people around the world, your day is already jam-packed. It probably looks something like this:

You wake up, earlier than you'd like, because there is a clock with a noise coming out of it that jolts you out of the sleep you want and need, into the day you have to face. You hit the shower, race through your morning routine, think about having breakfast, though you likely will either skip it or drink something that you call breakfast.

Now, if you have younger children like my wife and I have, you can multiply the chaos and rush of the morning. You have to make sure the children get out of bed and remind them several times to brush ALL of their teeth before they leave for school. You give them breakfast, because "breakfast is the most important meal of the day," and the irony that you just skipped it is something to be ignored because you just don't have the time to eat – at least not at home anyway. Maybe you'll grab something in the drive-through and eat it in the car.

Finally you hit the road, running a little later than you would like. The children are dropped off at school, the car gets gas, and other miscellaneous errands are taken care of on the way to work. The drive probably takes twice as long as it would take if there were no traffic hindering your progress.

You walk into work acutely aware of the fact you didn't get everything done yesterday, so there is far more work waiting for you than you can get done today. You think about how nice it would be to finally get caught up, but then you quickly dismiss that as an unrealistic fantasy.

Work is just that, work. You may enjoy your job, but if you're like most people, when asked, you can quickly describe what you would rather be doing. If you are like me and you love what you do, so much the better! Either way you blaze through the day, sometimes remembering to have lunch, sometimes not.

At 5 pm, you think about leaving, but try to push out that last bit of work to get caught up. Sometime between 5 and 6 pm you realize it's hopeless, and thus you surrender to the desire to go home. You sit in traffic again and ask yourself where all these people are going. You listen to some music to help you relax, but for some reason you frequently turn to talk radio, which only serves to get you more worked up than you already feel.

You walk in the door of your house to find everything is not as peaceful as you'd like. Bills need to be paid, dinner needs to be made or eaten, and someone has to do the dishes. By the time the evening chores are done, all you can bring yourself to do is fall on the couch.

You surf the internet or else turn on the TV. Maybe you catch the news, maybe some sports, maybe you watch the travel channel and wish you were somewhere, anywhere, but where you are.

Finally, after a couple hours, you drag yourself to bed, desperately trying to ignore the fact that you have to get up tomorrow and do this all over again.

The only break in this time-destroying routine is the weekend. Then again, if you are like most everyone else out there, Saturday and Sunday quickly pass by in a blur of over-commitment, involving hours of driving for children or family activities, not to mention attending church or other social commitments. You pack everything you can and more into those two days of "freedom from work."

By Sunday night you're exhausted. You'd like a vacation to recover from the weekend, but instead you'll get up just a little earlier than you'd like on Monday and start the routine all over again.

Did You Think, *This Sounds a Lot Like my Life*?

I may have described your life accurately, or maybe it's some variation on this theme. Do you ask yourself, in those rare moments of silence, what you are doing with your life and what mark you will leave on the world? Do you measure the quality and richness of your life and find yourself constantly saying things will get better in a few years?

Is your present life the one you want to live? More importantly, is this the life your Lord and Creator designed for you?

I know as well as anyone we all are under more time pressure than ever before. Life moves at a faster pace than it did even 20 years ago, and yet some things take longer. After all, consider the following:

According to the U. S. Department of Labor, the average American spends 2.6 hours a day watching television. The U. S. Census Bureau tells us the average American spends more than 100 hours a year commuting to work. *Time* magazine reports we are cramming more activity into the same amount of time by multitasking when it states, "modern parents multitask about 40 more hours a week than did their counterparts in 1975."

We also work harder at play. We have become obsessed with our hobbies. We overindulge in money and time at an alarming rate on so-called leisure activities to the point where they consume what little time we have left just to truly unwind and decompress.

Efficiency experts say we spend nine minutes a day waiting for computer files and Internet screens to download. We spend close to an hour a day just waiting in general. Don't get me started on the amount of time spent sitting at red lights, reading junk mail, or watching television commercials.

The tragedy in all of this is that we have forgotten how to be still. We have lost the art of sitting on the front porch, drinking a glass of lemonade, and listening to the wind move through the trees. We spend very little time opening up the Bible and reading the Word of God or praying to the God who created us. But who has time for that! Frankly, I'm impressed that you've even made it this far into the book.

So what's so important about how we spend our time anyway?

I've heard it said, you can measure someone's heart by looking through their checkbook and their calendar. How we spend our money and how we spend our time is a clear indicator of where our heart is.

The Bible goes so far as to use money as a comparison to God in our lives. You can only serve one master, either God or money (Matthew 6:24).

Consider this Question: What's Really more Valuable, Money or Time?

While you consider that question, here's another one. If I gave you a million dollars in exchange for you giving me 40 years of your life, would you take the money? No chance! Most people would agree time is more valuable than money.

You can always earn more money, but when you whittle away time in your life, it's gone and can never be regained. The Lord even asks the question, "Who among you can add even one day to your life?" Our lives are finite, and as the years go by we become more aware of this reality.

You've probably heard it said many times that when someone is on their deathbed they usually don't bemoan how much money they had, or what material possessions they missed. Instead, people have regrets about how they spent their time -- too much time at work and not enough time with the family. They regret that they never devoted time to accomplishing that great work that was in their hearts. Oliver Wendell Holmes is quoted as saying "most people die with their music still in them."

Matthew 6:21 reads, "Where your treasure is, there will your heart be also." Where is your treasure? Where have you invested your time? What is the great work still buried within you?

Where Your Treasure Is …

Let us consider where you have invested your treasure, your time.

The average American spends only 38.5 minutes in meaningful conversation with their children each week, according to the American Family Research Council. Focus on the Family reports that we spend only three minutes in conversation with our spouse each day.

There's an old story about a frightened little boy who was lying in bed one night listening to a thunderstorm. The lightning flashed and the thunder rumbled. Finally, he fled and jumped into his parents' bed.

His mother suggested he get back in his bed and talk to God to calm himself. His timeless reply was, "I need to talk to someone with skin on." Sometimes we just need someone with skin. I think we all can agree in the abstract that it is easier to talk with or relate to someone standing in front of us than it is to talk with our God.

So my question for you is, if you aren't spending time with the people you love, who you can see and touch, what will compel you to spend more time with the Lord?

Do you think I'm off base in posing this question? Ask yourself how much time you spent in one-on-one communication with God last week. While you ponder this, let's look at some facts about Christians and their time.

According to the American Religious Identification Survey of 2001, 77% of Americans say they are Christian. However, when we look at the survey on time use from the Bureau of Labor Statistics, we discover the average American spends only three minutes a day on religious activities.

Even worse, of the reported 77% of the population who say they are Christian, only 4.4% report spending any time at all in religious activities on a day other than Sunday. Those 4.4% report an average of just over one hour a day spent on religious activities.

On Sunday it's much better; the average American spends 33 minutes on religious activities. The percentage of Americans who report spending time in this area on Sunday is only 26%. Of that 26%, the average time spent on religious activities on Sunday was 2.1 hours.

This means less than 5% of the country spends more than 2.1 hours in an entire week focused on any kind of religious activity. Somewhere around 20% of the country spends about two hours a week, and the other 75% of Americans spend virtually no time at all!

How much time did you spend (with no other distractions) just reading the Bible, talking to the Lord in prayer, or in any other way having your focus totally and completely on God?

Are you okay with your answer to the last question? Do you think God is pleased with the amount of time you spend with Him on a daily or weekly basis? Are you pleased with your current relationship with God? Do you think He is?

How is your Relationship with the Lord?

How would you describe your relationship with God? How should it be described?

Listen to the words of Paul in Ephesians 5:32: "The two shall become one flesh. This is a great mystery for I speak of Christ and the church."

The Lord has given marriage to us as an example of what our relationship with Him should be like. Every Christian I've ever met would agree the priority of our relationships on this earth should be God first, our spouse second, our children third, followed by our extended family members, and then everyone else.

Let's start with marriage as an example of what our relationship with God can be. How would you describe an ideal relationship with your spouse?

When I think about the times I would rate my relationship with my wife as being the best it could possibly be, it is the times when I most feel we have "become one."

It is at those times when she's on my mind all the time. When I'm not with her, I can't wait to see her again. When she walks into a room my eyes sparkle and my heart feels more at peace. I sit and talk with her. Sometimes when she's not speaking, I can truly read her mind.

At those times I'll share myself with her and tell her my deepest thoughts, fears, hopes, and dreams, not because I expect her to fulfill them, but because I want her to know me better. I become sensitive to her needs, and look for little ways to show her how special she is to me.

Hopefully, that resonates with you on some level, but the most important question is, does that describe your relationship with the Lord?

I know, I know, that's not really fair is it? I mean we all felt like that when we first came to know the Lord, when we couldn't wait to sit down with the Word or listen to praise songs about Him. But as time goes by, passion can dissipate, just as in marriage the intensity of your feelings in courtship change as your marriage ages.

Anyone who still has a great marriage after a reasonable number of years can tell you it isn't always great, and it doesn't get or stay that way without constant effort and investment. That investment is time.

Do you believe you know God's will for your life? Without hesitation or doubt, do you know what God wants for you right now? How about hearing His voice? Does God speak to you on a regular basis? Do you hear His still, small voice when you are quiet in your soul, just as He says you will in His word?

Do you feel like He hears your prayers? Are you confident He is listening, and responding to you when you pray? Does God answer your prayers regardless of whether the answer is yes or no?

How much time are you spending in the Word each day? How about each week? Are you spending *any* time in the Word or in prayer? Do you think there is a connection between the questions in these last three paragraphs and how you feel about your relationship with the Lord?

Let's wrap up this section with a few questions for you to consider carefully and then answer. Score yourself on each question. Give yourself a 1 if the sentence does not describe you at all and a 10 if it describes you perfectly. Write your score beside each statement.

• I feel close to God. _____

• God speaks to me and I hear His voice. _____

• My life is going the direction God wants it to. _____

• God is pleased with how I use my time. _____

• God has placed a great work in my heart that I am here to accomplish and I know what it is. _____

• God would say that I put Him first in my life. _____

• I am happy with the amount of time I spend with the Lord. _____

• Instead of leaning on my own understanding, I trust the Lord to direct my path. _____

• The fruit of the spirit (love, joy, peace, patience, kindness, goodness, self-control) is strongly present in my life. _____

• Others see Christ in me and comment on the differences in my life compared to when I wasn't a Christian. _____

Total up your score and write it here: _____

80-100 It seems you have a wonderful relationship with the Lord. You'll love this book because it will provide a structure for you to spend more time with the Lord and cherish the relationship you already have.

60-80 Your walk and relationship with God are going in the right direction, but you sense neither are where they should be, and you may not be certain as to how to get where you know God wants you to be. This book will help you grow in your relationship with God and encourage you to really draw near to Him and better hear His voice and calling on your life.

40-60 You are not in a good place with God. If you have been near to Him in the past, consider this score as a warning you are falling away from the walk and relationship He wants to have with you. This book will help you refocus yourself on Him, as well as help you elevate Him to the position in your life He asks for and requires.

20-40 With a score in this range, it is clear that you are miles apart from God and His plan for your life. You may even struggle at times to remember what it was like when you were first saved. You may be at a point where you're doubting your faith or thinking of divorcing yourself from the Lord. This book can help you return to your first love. It will help you remember why you came to the Lord to begin with and will get you moving in the right direction on an eternal level. However, you really should spend some time with your pastor and a strong Christian friend. Share with them your answer to the assessment above.

0-20 Are you truly a born-again Christian? If you are at this low point in your life, you probably feel like you've hit rock bottom. You may wonder where God is in all of this, if He even cares about you. Answer this question honestly -- If you were to die today, are you 100% certain that you would go to heaven? If you are not sure, then you need to *seek out a pastor or Christian friend immediately*. This book is not the right one for you to read if you are uncertain about where you will spend eternity (whether in heaven or hell), because this is the most important issue you must first address in your life.

If you are certain you will spend eternity in heaven with the Lord, then you need to spend time with a pastor or friend to share with them what is going on in your life. Maybe you haven't wanted to share these things with anyone because you've thought no one would understand. You can always be sure of one thing: God knows, and Jesus understands.

Jesus lived and died so that He could understand what you're going through, and to save your soul from hell. Share this assessment with a pastor or Christian friend, and ask them to counsel you through the issues you are facing. This is a time in your life when you need someone to help hold you up and be strong for you.

Does God need your time? Of course He doesn't *need* it. But God desires your time because it represents *your life*, and you touch His heart when you spend it with Him. God created us to have a relationship with Him. He's waiting for you to give Him your time and your heart.

Two
How are You Really Spending your Time?

It is interesting how we view ourselves and how we determine what is reality. For example, when the story about Barry Bonds' steroid use was playing out in the news, the following results were obtained from a survey conducted concerning steroid use among teen athletes: 10% of high school students thought some of the athletes at their school were using steroids, and 25% thought athletes at a *rival* school were using steroids.

I find it ironic (but very revealing of human nature) people thought hardly anyone at their school would do something like that, but students were more than twice as likely to think someone at a different school would do it.

Transferring this thought process to how most Americans are spending their time, now it's time to ask this question: how do you think you are spending yours?

In the professional world, I'm a financial planner. I run a moderately sized financial planning firm in Orange County, California. One of the things I spend a lot of time doing is helping parents design financial strategies to pay for their kids' college education.

In these conversations I invariably ask the question, "How much money can you comfortably afford to set aside every month to save for future college expenses?" Regardless of the answer given, I probe a little deeper.

Let's say the client said they could save $1000 a month. Then I'll look at their home equity line of credit and ask, "How much did you owe at this time last year?" Then I'll take a look at their credit card balances and ask the same question.

More often than not I find their debt is increasing every year, which means they really can't afford to save $1000 a month. In fact, in almost 25% of the situations I find they are already spending more than they are making. So the monthly "savings" is really just debt they would incur in other areas.

In finances, the little things add up. Most people have a black hole in their budget into which 20% of their money goes. They know they had that money at one time, but they don't know how or where they spent it. Furthermore, they don't really have anything to show for it.

Likewise, people also have a black hole in their schedule. At the end of every week they know they had the time to get everything on their to-do list done, and they know they did something with their time, but they don't really have anything to show for it. It's just gone and they aren't sure where it went.

In your schedule, where are your black holes? In money, it is discretionary purchases, cash expenditures, and things that are charged to a credit card or line of credit. In your schedule it can be reading the paper, surfing the Internet, or doing any number of nonproductive, time-wasting tasks.

Whatever it is, these black holes, or time sinks, drain your time without providing you with any real benefit. It's like eating a nice dessert in a restaurant. For the five minutes you are eating, you fully enjoy the experience, but it provides you nothing of lasting value. If anything, it's adding unnecessary calories and subtracting well-earned money from your wallet!

Let me pose a few questions for you to ponder, and then I want you to make an educated guess as to the answer as it applies to your life. What percentage of the time in your life are you spending on black holes -- things that may provide some minor enjoyment for the moment, but are of no real value to your life? Write in your estimate of the percentage of your time you think you are wasting here: _____

If you are unsatisfied with where you are at this point in your life, in your walk with the Lord, or in what you are doing with the one life He has given you to live, then I would like to propose the following challenge:

Give God a Tithe of your Time for the Next 40 Days

What I have just proposed is so radical, so terrifying, and so potentially life-altering you probably just experienced an almost overwhelming desire to put this book down and never pick it up again!

If you just experienced that feeling, it's your flesh, the sin nature in you, stepping up and saying this is a terrible idea. But let it sit for a while, and wait to see what the Lord says. Let's talk about what I've suggested and why.

A tithe is 10%, usually of your earnings, which is given as an acknowledgement that none of it belongs to us. God provides everything for us, and He asks us to give 10% back to Him through the tithe. In so doing, it is as if we are giving Him everything.

In the Bible the tithe is called the "first fruits," meaning the best of what we have been given. God asked the Hebrews to give Him the best of their harvest or to sacrifice an unblemished lamb -- not the scraps or the leftovers, but the best.

God tells us He can do more for us with the 90% we have left than we can do for ourselves with the 100% that we started out with. Do you believe this? In the book of Malachi in the Old Testament, God even challenges us to test Him in our giving, and He promises that we cannot out-give Him.

In nothing else does God ask us to test Him, but in the area of giving Him our tithes, He tells us to do just that. Tithing is an act of faith. It requires faith to give away 10% of our money when we can think of so many other things we could do with those dollars. But in faith we are trusting God to make up the difference and then some.

Now let me be clear. I am not saying the Bible tells you to test God by tithing of your time and that He will out-give you. I am saying tithing your time lines up perfectly with the precepts of God's Word. No one can debate that God desires our time and attention.

He wants to be first in your life, and He wants to spend time with you. Do you think that God, the Creator of the universe, can do more with the 90% of your time left after tithing it to Him than you can do with the 100%? Of course He can.

Every day has 24 hours, and a week has 168 hours. I am literally suggesting you tithe 2.4 hours a day -- 16.8 hours a week -- to God, and devote those hours wholly to Him. To spending time with Him in prayer and in His Word, as well as in worship and praise, with your attention completely and totally focused on Him.

I'm suggesting you do that every day for 40 days. By making this suggestion I am saying if you give that time to God for the next 40 days, you *will* draw closer to Him. His word promises this. "Draw near to God and He will draw near to you" (James 4:8).

I'm saying if you give God 10% of your time, it is just as if you've given Him the whole 100%. It is truly a tithe of time.

Is this Biblical?

God does not say anywhere in the Bible that we must spend 10% of our time with Him, but this is a biblical principal. Some will want to debate if tithing is continued in the New Testament or not. Either way, it is still a biblical principal. Do you truly believe the Lord will not honor you for putting Him first in your life?

Do you believe God is asking you to slow down your life enough to give Him a tithe of your time for 40 days? Take a moment to put this book down right now and ask Him. I'd be willing to guess that He will answer you in your spirit even as you are asking the question.

So here's the bottom line: If you believe in your heart that God is asking you to do this, to give Him this tithe of time for 40 days, then you need to do it. If you do not, it becomes a sin issue simply because God has asked you to do something.

How many times have you said, "If God would just tell me what to do I would do it"? If you've ever said that concerning how to make time for Him in your life, then here you are. This is where you're put to the test. God has told you what to do; are you going to do it?

If you need a little more convincing, here's something to consider: the Bible says that we are to have no other gods before Him. It's one of the Ten Commandments. Is there something you are spending your time on that is becoming a god in your life -- something that is challenging Him for your attention and adoration?

Jesus tells us in the gospels that we are to love the Lord our God with all our heart, soul, mind, and strength (Mark 12:30 and Luke 10:27). Jesus says this is the greatest commandment. How you spend your time is certainly a reflection of your heart and soul and mind. Does how you spend your time tell God you love Him with ALL of your heart, soul, and mind?

Is God first in your schedule? If He isn't, then how can He really be first in your life? Let me ask the earlier question again: Do you believe God is asking you to slow down your life enough to give Him a tithe of your time for 40 days?

What we are really talking about here is taking an opportunity to simply slow down … to pause from the stress and pressure of life … to take your mind off the temporal … to put your full attention, just for 40 days, on the eternal. In essence, taking a vacation from life and visiting heaven for those 40 days.

This will be a time of refreshing. This is a fundamental biblical concept, and it is central to one of the most well-known psalms, Psalm 23: "The Lord is my shepherd; I shall not want." A good shepherd is in control of the sheep. "He makes me to lie down in green pastures." This isn't a suggestion or a choice. The Lord doesn't ask us if we would like to lie down, He compels us -- *makes* us -- lie down. It's almost as if He knows what we need. Imagine that! Then, only after these things have been affirmed, "He leads me beside the still waters." Again, He is leading us, directing us, taking us where we need to go. All of this leads up to this next section of scripture.

"He restores my soul." Isn't that what we want? When we are tired and beaten down by life; when we feel like it's never going to be the way we want it to be and our soul is weary, "He restores [our] my soul." Could it be that we have become so busy with life we've lost the time to really *live*?

When was the last time the Lord made you lie down? When has He led you beside still waters? God doesn't change, and He does not fail us. If He has been saying these things to you, could it be you aren't listening? Could it be that He has been trying to get your attention for a very long time and that He is waiting beside the still waters to restore your soul?

Take a moment right now to lie down in the green pastures ... to sit beside Him next to the still waters. Just talk with Him. Write down your thoughts to Him as if you were going to send Him a letter. Open up to Him; begin, right now, to draw near. Just let the words flow. If you get stuck, start by thanking Him for specific things He has done in your life.

_____

_____

_____

_____

_____

_____

_____

_____

_____

_____

_____

_____

_____

_____

_____

_____

_____

_____

How do You Currently Spend your Time?

The first step in learning how to tithe your time is to create an estimate of how you currently spend your time. Use the estimated time usage sheet provided below. The average American's time usage for each daily activity listed below is in parentheses; on the spaces provided, write your own estimated time percentages.

Work Related (8.2 hours) _____

Sleeping (7.6 hours) _____

Miscellaneous (4.6 hours) _____

Recreational (2.6 hours) _____

Household Activities (1 hour) _____

God Related (.05 hours) _____

Next, we are going to directly assess how you actually spend your time, and then we will go back and compare your estimates with the actual results. Remember, it's not important where your time is being spent right now. Knowing what you are actually doing is what we are after because that will be the foundation for creating our plan.

At my financial planning firm, I will occasionally have my entire staff complete a time analysis. The purpose is to look closely at what we are spending our time on and to discover opportunities to increase the value of what we do. The way I do it is simple.

Make seven copies of the Time Sheet you will find in the back of the book. Your assignment for the next week is to track how you use your time in 15-minute increments. Simply stop what you're doing every 15 minutes and write the letter on the sheet that represents the activity you've been doing most for the past 15 minutes.

At the end of the seven-day period you're tracking, take the sheets and tally up the amount of time spent in each subcategory. Then add those together to calculate the time spent in each of the six main categories.

Now calculate the percentage of time spent. The formula to do that is simple. There are 168 hours in a week. Divide the number of hours spent in each category by 168. The result is the percentage of time spent in that category. Calculate the percentage of time spent for the six main categories as well as for each subcategory.

Now the challenge is to carve out the time you will give to the Lord. To do this you must either create new time by getting up earlier or staying up later, or you must replace activities you are currently spending time on.

Remember this is only for 40 days. No one is asking you to give up anything permanently, just for the next 40 days. Jesus fasted for 40 days, so I think you and I can give up some TV or golfing time in order to draw closer to our Father and Maker.

During the week, while assessing your time, think about the questions below:

• If God were your "life boss" and brought you in for an evaluation of how you spend your time, what would He say?

• What does God want you to accomplish with your life? What has the Lord uniquely gifted you to do?

• What do you want to accomplish with your life? What passion or fire is in your heart?

• Why are you reading this book?

• What one thing do you want the Lord to do/change/speak to you during this time?

• Write an example of the time in your life when the Lord spoke to you most clearly. Where were you? What were you doing? How did He speak to you? What did He say?

• Write your obituary. When you die (since the statistics are heavily in favor of all of us experiencing death), what do you want someone to say at your memorial service? Write out what you would want written or spoken about you. Here is what I wrote:

Today we are here to remember and celebrate the life of William Jordan. William was a husband, a father, a business owner, an active member of his church, and a valuable member of the community. More than anything else, William was a Christian who clearly placed God above all else. William modeled Christ in his life to his wife, his family, and everyone who knew him. He made an impact for the Lord during his lifetime here on earth. He shared his faith with others, gave generously, and helped to build others in their faith. William strove to be a good husband, and even after more than sixty years of marriage would still read books on being a better husband and would attend conferences and workshops to improve himself. William helped raise two daughters and was deeply proud of the women they grew to be. In turn they married and raised families of their own, passing on the legacy of God's faithfulness and blessings to another generation. In work, William's business made a positive impact on the community. He helped thousands of families accomplish their most important financial and life goals. He educated his clients on the more important things in life: he helped them realize they are here for a purpose, and to identify their purpose. From an eternal perspective, William wrote a book, *A Tithe of Time*, which transformed millions of lives around the world. When it was time to leave this earth behind, William peacefully laid down his body here, knowing his Father in heaven was waiting to welcome him into eternity.

[Please note: I don't think I have successfully completed any of the items listed above. Each and every one is a journey that I will finish only when I have drawn my last breath. However, Lord willing, these are the goals I aspire to and by the grace of God will accomplish.]

• What are your goals for your life for the next year, 5 years, 10, and 20 years? This question should demonstrate what you want/need to do in order to be moving towards the life goals you will write down in your obituary. Take some time right now to make a list of the most important things you would want in your obituary. Then write it out below.

Three
Success Begins with a Plan

Let's get down to business. You've assessed your time for the last week and are ready to begin. However, you can't just cram an extra two and a half hours into your schedule; therefore, you first need to free up some time from your schedule and then replace it with these hours.

Look at the assessment and start flagging the areas you are willing to reduce and then replace for just forty days. Anyone can replace something from his or her schedule for forty days. If you can't, you probably need to ask yourself whether or not that irreplaceable thing is becoming a god in your life. Remember, you are doing this to create time for God. Let's see what the Lord will do.

In the previous week you were praying about this and asking for the Lord's leading. During this week you need to listen to the leading of the Holy Spirit and let go of the things that are not essential to your weekly routine.

Write out the times each day you will spend with the Lord. Use the time sheet included in this book and write in your times. If each week will not be the same, make copies of the time sheet so that you have enough for all six weeks. It is important to fill in this time first before you add anything else to your schedule. If you don't put this time in first, you'll find that it just slips through your fingers. Life gets busy and it is easy to forget. By writing it down, you are prioritizing this block of time in your mind and on paper, and sealing your commitment to God in offering Him that time.

Another option for creating additional time in your day is by getting up earlier or staying up later. Personally, I love to sleep in as late as I can. In my house that unfortunately translates into getting up around 6:30 am, but if I could sleep until 8 I probably would.

Can I get up an hour earlier for forty days to create some additional time for the Lord? Of course I can. Might I be a little tired? Probably. Can God do more with a tired servant totally focused on Him than with a well-rested man going about his own business? You better believe it!

In this, as in all things, seek the Lord's will and His leading. I once shared with a friend of mine that I was trying to get up earlier in the day but was struggling with it. I felt I was sinning because God had told me to get up earlier and it was really difficult for me to do.

My friend asked me if I *truly believed* God cared what time I got up. Without hesitation my answer was a strong, "Yes!" because I felt certain the Lord had spoken that to me. He speaks to each of us individually. What is He speaking to you?

While we are on the subject of prayer, you must be in prayer over this process from the day you consider it until the day you complete it. Paul tells us to "pray without ceasing" in 1 Thessalonians 5:17. In Ephesians 6:18 Paul says to "pray always." This Tithe of Time six-week plan is a great opportunity to practice this kind of prayer.

Ask the Lord to prepare your heart and your mind to hear His voice. Ask Him to draw you closer to Himself to help you focus your heart and soul on His voice. Ask that He would guard your time and lead you to the quiet pastures and still waters to commune with Him!

Can I Just Do this for a Few Days or a Week?

For many people the thought of making a forty-day commitment is daunting and they're convinced they won't be able to stick with it. Keep in mind this is a normal gut reaction by your flesh; your flesh is trying to reduce the commitment you are making to something which seems a little more comfortable. Don't let it win! You *can* do this!

There is compelling biblical reasoning for forty days. If you are a student of the Bible, you know numbers in scripture have a depth of meaning that goes beyond their numerical value. God uses forty days for testing, trials, and tribulation, but also for change and transformation, as well as reflection and refocusing. He also uses forty days to give us opportunities to follow His path, and to provide us with His correction when we do not follow. Many examples of the relevance of forty days in God's economy can be found all throughout Scripture.

Jesus spent forty days in the wilderness, as referenced in Mark's Gospel. Our Lord and Savior, the very Creator of the universe, took forty days to go off and be alone to commune with Himself in the form of the Trinity. What greater example could we ask for?

In Genesis chapter 7, the Lord sent rain upon the earth for forty days to cleanse it, preserving only Noah and his family as well as the animals aboard the ark. Later when He was preparing Moses to lead His people, we find a period of forty years had passed from when Moses fled Egypt to when the Lord appeared to him in the burning bush.

When Moses went up to Mount Sinai to receive the Ten Commandments, he was there with God for forty days. Twice, as the first time he broke the tablets in anger at the sin of the people. This was during the forty years Israel was led by Him in the wilderness. That period of time in the wilderness was directly preceded by the forty days the spies were in the land and came back too afraid of the inhabitants to trust God and take the land.

In chapters 3 and 5 of the book of Judges we read, "the land had rest forty years." Later in the time of King Saul, Goliath came and challenged Israel for forty days. In the book of Psalms we're told that the Lord grieved for forty years. The prophet Ezekiel refers to Egypt being empty for forty years as a judgment of the Lord.

In the book of Jonah, the Lord tells him to give the people of Nineveh forty days to repent of their sins. Finally in the Gospels we read Jesus appeared to His disciples for forty days following His death and resurrection before He ascended into heaven.

I think we can agree forty days is the right amount of time!

How to Spend your Time During the Forty Days

First of all, I want you to think about what you will do with this extra time. Don't worry; I'll help you with this. We just don't want to spend the time lying on the couch or in bed, or wandering aimlessly in the park. We want to dedicate this time to the Lord and use it as He directs.

As a result, you will find this book to be different from most you have read. My goal is to give you a framework within which you can ask the Lord to lead you. Ultimately, submit to the Lord what you will do with this time, and follow His direction and leading.

There are seven areas you can spend your time in:
o Bible study
o Prayer
o Meditation
o Worship
o Scripture memorization
o Attending church
o Something else the Lord is putting on your heart?

These should be the singular focus of your allotted time and not simply activities you accomplish while getting something else done as a good multitasker. For instance, listening to the Bible on tape/CD while driving (which isn't a bad thing at all) should not count. You can't interact with God while you have to focus on driving. Instead, if you choose to spend that time in prayer, the only thing you should be doing is praying.

1. Bible Study – This book can serve as a guide for your study, as well as a template that you can use should you repeat this Tithe of Time process again.

2. Prayer – When is the last time you really spent quality time in prayer? If you are like me, and most Christians, prayer usually means 30 seconds before meals or bed. Spend time, and I mean real time such as thirty or even sixty minutes, fellowshipping with the Lord in prayer. Confess your sins and seek forgiveness. Restoring your spirit before the Lord so you are clean. As the Lord leads, you might consider combining prayer with fasting.

3. Meditation – While similar to prayer, this is spending time dwelling on a more focused thought or verse, not the eastern forms of meditation where you only try to empty your mind. Rather, this is the meditation spoken of in the Word. Read Joshua 1:8, Psalm 1:2, and 1 Timothy 4:15. Biblically mandated meditation involves completely focusing your attention on one or more verses. Don't just say them over and over like some mindless mantra, but really explore them with the Lord and ask Him to open those verses up to you in your life.

4. Worship – I was tempted to include a worship CD with this book. However, not everyone will share my taste in music. Simply grab a worship CD from your church or from one or more of your favorite Christian artists. Spend time participating (not just listening) in worship, singing to the Lord. Remember, the Psalms repeatedly tell us to "make a joyful noise" to the Lord. The Bible doesn't say you have to be skilled -- just joyful! Music was given to us as a gift from God, and for most people, worship music brings them into the presence of God.

5. Scripture Memorization – David says, "Thy word have I hid in my heart that I might not sin against thee" (Psalm 119:11). What verse or verses will the Lord bring to you to memorize now, so they are hidden in your heart when the day of temptation comes?

6. Attending Church – If your church is like most, you could probably attend two, three, or even more services a week. God tells us not to forsake gathering together, and this is a great way to focus your attention on the Lord.

7. Something Else – Ask God specifically what He wants you to do during this time. I can't guess the variety of ways the Lord might lead you to spend your time. Above all, listen to His leading.

Take some time now to make some notes on how you will spend your time, and how *much* time you will spend in any or all of these areas. Once that's finished, take your plan and write down the ways you will spend your time in the specific time slots you have allocated for your Tithe of Time.

Now comes the final step. Share the plan with your spouse and/or at least one close friend. Try to get them to do this with you for support and encouragement. Whenever you set a goal to achieve anything in life, your best chances for success are when you make yourself accountable to someone else for the commitments you have made.

Success Tips

1. Carry this book with you and keep it where you can see it at all times during the next forty days. It will be a visible reminder of your commitment, and you'll also have the daily tracking sheets provided in the book readily at hand for when you need them.

2. Get a 15-minute kitchen timer or a watch with a timer. Use it while you are recording your 15-minute increments of time so you don't forget. If you do forget, catch up as soon as you remember.

3. Categorize the use of time right then and there, before it slips your mind. Don't think you can wait until the end of the day to fill in time assessments. It's not going to happen.

4. Find a partner who would like to do his or her own Tithe of Time along with you. Ideally, this would be your spouse or a best friend. However, anyone you know could be a partner. Keep each other focused on honoring your time commitments. This book could be read and implemented with your small fellowship or Bible study group. If you have one, go through this together as a small community of believers. The fellowship and accountability will help protect you and carry you through. It will encourage and strengthen you to see the changes in others and for them to see what God is doing in your life!

Here we go! I promise you this: If you give your Creator, Father, and Lord a Tithe of Time for the next forty days, you will never be the same!

Four
A Tithe of Time, Week One

As we begin your Tithe of Time for the next 40 days, let's begin with a discussion of the format. First of all, feel free to deviate from the format any time the Lord leads you to! All I've done is create a rough framework of two pages for each day to help you structure your time. Should God pull you in a different way, follow Him, not me!

When that happens, and it will, take the time to record what happened in some of the space provided here. For a number of reasons, you will want a record of what is happening. There is a lot of room to write, but if you need more space, use a journal.

For a framework to this study, I have used the book of James. For a period of more than two years, God beat me over the head with this book and told me to study it and use it here! If at any time during the next 40 days God directs you to a different book, follow Him.

The Lord says in Hebrews 4:12 that the Bible is "living and powerful, and sharper than any two edged sword." Combine that with the fact that God is doing different things in His relationship with you, and He may direct you in a different way than he directed me.

Should you find yourself wanting to go through the Tithe of Time a second time, here's all you need to do:

Start with whatever book of the Bible God directs you to. Divide it into 5 sections of chapters. Then further divide each section into 7 subsections of scriptures. It could be just 2-5 verses a day, or it could be an entire chapter a day. Simple enough.

The theme for the week and day should come out of those scriptures. If you have a Bible that has section headings, it can be easier to see where the natural breaks are and to get a sense of what the themes will be. However, you can identify the themes on a daily basis as you go along.

For the word study, let the scriptures lead you. You can read the scripture for the day and simply let God pull something out for you. If He doesn't pull you in one specific direction, then pick a key word and study it.

Make sure you do this daily even if it isn't a strong compulsion. Repetition can often create a pattern or habit God can use at a different time. What seems boring one day can turn into a profound and moving experience in an instant.

Lastly, I have provided room for writing your thoughts, experiences and impressions. This is a way of both speaking with the Lord and recording where He is taking you. I know you may not like to write, but you need to do this faithfully. This is a critical component of our plan. Please do not skip it!

In the first week of our study, our theme from the book of James will be choice. You have already exercised your choice in life by choosing to sacrifice some of "your" time and tithe it to God for forty days. I want to make a quick comment about this, and the concept of "your" time.

For years, one of my greatest pet peeves was someone "stealing my time" by asking me to be somewhere at a certain time, and then being late. If I showed up for a business event, a church function, or whatever, and it started more than a few minutes late, I became upset and felt the person involved was stealing time from me.

While there is truth to this (and we should all make an effort not to steal time from someone else), I recently had a revelation. *It's not my time!* It's God's time. I can accept everything I have is God's. When I came to the realization my time belonged to God and didn't belong to me, it was one of the most shocking and freeing moments of my life. If I was where God wanted me, then it was up to Him how my time would be used. So use God's time, as a good steward, always remembering none of it really belongs to you anyway!

Week #: **1**   Day #: **1**   Today's Date: _____

Chapter for the Week: **James 1**   Verse for today: **1**

Theme for the Week: **choice**   Theme for the Day: **servanthood**

Word Study for Today: **bondservant**   Psalm for Today: **Psalm 1**

Memory verse for the week: **James 1:19-21**

For this book, I could have selected any of the 66 books of the Bible. All scripture is God breathed and useful for teaching, rebuking, correcting and training in righteousness (2 Timothy 3:16). So why the book of James?

God has been pulling me back to this book for more than four years. As we go through the next forty days, you will see why. I know God will speak to you as He has to me, though probably with different specifics.

James has been a book that has challenged me to live out my faith, not just experience it as intellectual knowledge or in a passive way. James jumps right into this with the very first verse, describing himself as a bondservant.

We know from scripture Jesus Himself came "not to be served but to serve". Matt 20:28 and Mark 10:45. During the time of Jesus, the difference between a servant and a bondservant was significant. A servant was compelled to serve and was without choice. However a bondservant was someone who had chosen of their own free will to submit themselves to being a servant.

So which was Jesus? Obviously He was a bondservant. No one could compel Jesus, but He freely chose to come to us to serve. His entire ministry was one of servanthood, culminating with the private act of washing His disciples' feet when none of them would lower themselves to do so, and His ultimate public act of service in freely laying down His life for ours.

Imagine yourself having your feet washed by our Lord. As your Savior and King washes your feet, what act of service is He asking of you?

Specific time spent with the Lord today and what was done:

_____

_____

Write out the memory verse for the week:

_____

_____

_____

_____

_____

In your own words, write about what the Lord is saying to you through the Verses for today:

_____

_____

_____

_____

_____

How do the Theme for the Day and/or Week apply to your life now?

_____

_____

_____

_____

_____

_____

As you were studying the word for today, what did you learn or discover?

_____

_____

_____

_____

_____

_____

Using the psalm you read today as a guide, write your own psalm to the Lord from your own heart:

_____

_____

_____

_____

_____

_____

_____

_____

_____

_____

Prayer requests and/or prayers answered (share with your Father from your heart):

_____

_____

_____

_____

_____

_____

What else is the Lord putting on your heart today?

_____

_____

_____

_____

_____

_____

What other scriptures did you read today that were most impactful? How did they speak to you?

_____

_____

_____

_____

_____

Week #: **1**   Day #: **2**   Today's Date: _____

Chapter for the Week: **James 1**   Verses for Today: **2-8**

Theme for the Week: **choice**   Theme for the Day: **trials**

Word Study for Today: **joy**   Psalm for Today: **Psalm 139**

When you woke up this morning, the first thing you asked the Lord for was to send you some trials today. Right?

Of course not. No one wants to experience trials and we certainly don't go around tempting God to put us through trials. And yet James tells us here not to simply push through our trials, but to actually consider it "pure joy". Wow!

We'd have to wonder what God was trying to tell us here, but thankfully He clarifies what He is saying, the "testing of your faith produces patience/perseverance/endurance (depending on your translation).

This word patience (King James) in the New Testament refers to someone who is not swayed from his specific decision to follow Christ regardless of the trials or tribulations he experiences.

In James, the Lord tells us patience will finish its work in us so we will be "perfect and complete". God is growing us through the trials we experience just as the refiner's fire is used to purify the metal that will be used for crafting some beautiful piece of work.

I love the point God communicates to us through the fiery furnace in the book of Daniel. We will face trials. But that's when God shows up. He doesn't usually come to us when we are walking along in peace and prosperity, thinking we are doing okay on our own.

No, the Lord stands by us in the fires and trials of life. Frankly, I wouldn't want it any other way. So while it's hard to celebrate your trials, fix your eyes on Him and recognize He is perfecting His work in you!

Specific time spent with the Lord today and what was done:

_____

_____

Write out the memory verse for the week:

_____

_____

_____

_____

_____

In your own words, write about what the Lord is saying to you through the Verses for today:

_____

_____

_____

_____

_____

_____

How do the Theme for the Day and/or Week apply to your life now?

_____

_____

_____

_____

_____

_____

As you were studying the word for today, what did you learn or discover?

_____

_____

_____

_____

_____

_____

Using the psalm you read today as a guide, write your own psalm to the Lord from your own heart:

_____

_____

_____

_____

_____

_____

_____

_____

_____

_____

_____

Prayer requests and/or prayers answered (share with your Father from your heart):

_____

_____

_____

_____

_____

_____

What else is the Lord putting on your heart today?

_____

_____

_____

_____

_____

_____

What other scriptures did you read today that were most impactful? How did they speak to you?

_____

_____

_____

_____

_____

Week #: **1**   Day #: **3**   Today's Date: _____

Chapter for the Week: **James 1**   Verses for Today: **9-11**

Theme for the Week: **choice**

Theme for the Day: **humble circumstances**

Word Study for Today: **glory**   Psalm for Today: **Psalm 3**

So often in this world, the focus and the "glory" goes to the person who has the most earthly wealth or riches. Isn't it wonderful these things mean nothing to God?

In this section, James tells us, rich or poor, we can rejoice in our situation. He goes so far as to tell the brother in "humble circumstances" to take pride in or "glory" in his situation.

Could it be because God has more opportunity to bless the brother in humble circumstances than the one who is rich in the things of this earth? How many times does our savings account or a credit card bail us out of trouble when God was preparing to show His power in our situation?

Now let's be clear the Lord, through James, is referring to both as brothers. It is clear one's financial status is not the determining factor in the status of our salvation. Praise God for that, regardless of your personal financial situation.

God is clear those in more humble circumstances find themselves in a higher position than those who would consider themselves rich. After all, how much easier is it to be truly thankful for the food before you, if you have actually lived through a time where you did not have enough to eat?

In America today, we should all think of ourselves as rich. If you go to bed at night with confidence in where your food for the next day will come from, you are better off than millions, maybe even billions of people in this world.

So glory in your situation, regardless of how God is blessing you.

Specific time spent with the Lord today and what was done:

_____

_____

Write out the memory verse for the week:

_____

_____

_____

_____

_____

In your own words, write about what the Lord is saying to you through the Verses for today:

_____

_____

_____

_____

_____

How do the Theme for the Day and/or Week apply to your life now?

_____

_____

_____

_____

_____

_____

As you were studying the word for today, what did you learn or discover?

_____

_____

_____

_____

_____

_____

_____

Using the psalm you read today as a guide, write your own psalm to the Lord from your own heart:

_____

_____

_____

_____

_____

_____

_____

_____

_____

_____

_____

Prayer requests and/or prayers answered (share with your Father from your heart):

_____

_____

_____

_____

_____

What else is the Lord putting on your heart today?

_____

_____

_____

_____

_____

What other scriptures did you read today that were most impactful? How did they speak to you?

_____

_____

_____

_____

_____

Week #: **1**   Day #: **4**   Today's Date: _____

Chapter for the Week: **James 1**   Verses for Today: **12-15**

Theme for the Week: **choice**   Theme for the Day: **temptation**

Word Study for Today: **desires**   Psalm for Today: **Psalm 38**

Every one of us will experience temptation. Here, God promises us a blessing when we endure temptation.

God says we are tempted by our desires or lusts. No one is tempted by something which is not a desire for them. So be prepared for temptation in the areas of your desires, your fleshly lusts.

What I find interesting is that it isn't the desire here that is sin. James says "after desire has conceived, it gives birth to sin". First the desire comes as temptation. Then, if we allow this desire to "conceive" it will give birth to sin.

Prepare for the temptation. You already know where it will often come from because those same desires will conceive in you and give birth to sin. However you also know when you experience temptation, 1 Cor. 10:13 tells us God will provide for you a way of escape.

We can look to Jesus for guidance with handling temptation. When Jesus was tempted by Satan, He went to the scriptures as His defense. David says he hid God's word in his heart that "I might not sin against God".

As part of your time spent with the Lord each day, spend time dedicated to both reading and memorizing scripture, especially when you find a scripture that helps you in an area you have struggled with or have been tempted in before. Write that scripture down and commit it to memory so you can call on it in your time of need.

Give praise to God when you experience temptation. Use scripture to overcome through the power of the Holy Spirit. Then rejoice, knowing that God has blessed you because you have endured temptation.

Specific time spent with the Lord today and what was done:

_____

_____

Write out the memory verse for the week:

_____

_____

_____

_____

_____

In your own words, write about what the Lord is saying to you through the Verses for today:

_____

_____

_____

_____

_____

_____

How do the Theme for the Day and/or Week apply to your life now?

_____

_____

_____

_____

_____

_____

_____

As you were studying the word for today, what did you learn or discover?

_____

_____

_____

_____

_____

_____

Using the psalm you read today as a guide, write your own psalm to the Lord from your own heart:

_____

_____

_____

_____

_____

_____

_____

_____

_____

_____

_____

Prayer requests and/or prayers answered (share with your Father from your heart):

_____

_____

_____

_____

_____

_____

What else is the Lord putting on your heart today?

_____

_____

_____

_____

_____

_____

What other scriptures did you read today that were most impactful? How did they speak to you?

_____

_____

_____

_____

_____

Week #: **1** Day #: **5** Today's Date: ____________

Chapter for the Week: **James 1** Verses for Today: **16-18**

Theme for the Week: **choice** Theme for the Day: **good gifts**

Word Study for Today: **gift** Psalm for Today: **Psalm 112**

Have you ever had a gift to give someone you were so excited about you could hardly contain yourself? For my oldest daughter's 10th birthday, we took her to see the musical Wicked. It's an adaptation of the classic musical The Wizard of Oz. She considers it one of the best nights of her life. I was so excited to take her to see that show.

God has gifts to give to us that He is very excited about. He knows just how to bless us, and what gifts to give to us. He is waiting for that special occasion or opportunity to give us good and perfect gifts.

Not just some gifts, but "every good and perfect gift is from above". From the simple foods we eat to the clothes we wear. He gives our health, our skills and talents, every day of our life is a gift from God.

Here the Bible refers to us as His first fruits of all creation. God loves us vastly more than we have the capacity to love our own children. Just as we desire to give good gifts and blessings to our children, He desires to give us even more.

Think about some special gifts you have given to those who you care about over the years. Remember the joy you experienced with the giving. Now imagine that your special gift was unwelcome or unused and unappreciated. Your excitement would quickly turn to sorrow.

The question is, what will you do with the gifts and talents from your God who loves you so deeply? How will you react to the gifts He gives you on a daily basis?

As you proceed through this study, ask the Lord what great work He has prepared for you to do for Him with the gifts He has given you.

Specific time spent with the Lord today and what was done:

____

____

Write out the memory verse for the week:

_____

_____

_____

_____

_____

In your own words, write about what the Lord is saying to you through the Verses for today:

_____

_____

_____

_____

_____

_____

How do the Theme for the Day and/or Week apply to your life now?

_____

_____

_____

_____

_____

_____

As you were studying the word for today, what did you learn or discover?

_____

_____

_____

_____

_____

_____

Using the psalm you read today as a guide, write your own psalm to the Lord from your own heart:

_____

_____

_____

_____

_____

_____

_____

_____

_____

_____

Prayer requests and/or prayers answered (share with your Father from your heart):

_____

_____

_____

_____

_____

_____

What else is the Lord putting on your heart today?

_____

_____

_____

_____

_____

_____

What other scriptures did you read today that were most impactful? How did they speak to you?

_____

_____

_____

_____

_____

Week #: **1**   Day #: **6**   Today's Date: _____

Chapter for the Week: **James 1**   Verses for today: **19-25**

Theme for the Week: **choice**

Theme for the Day: **doers of the word**

Word Study for Today: **doer**   Psalm for Today: **Psalm 31**

For centuries, Christians were the "doers" of the world. If you travel the globe, you will find countless hospitals, colleges and universities, mostly founded by Christians. If someone needed help, a Christian would be the person to call on. If others wouldn't do it, Christians would step in and make it happen.

Over the past century, that seems to be changing. We Christians seem content to sit in our churches, drop our donations in the offering basket, and let someone else do the heavy lifting.

People so often complain about the government with it's massive bureaucracies and waste. We rant and rave about how they can't get it right, and so often do more harm than good. But if we are honest with ourselves, the government has often stepped in to fill a void that should have been filled by Christians.

We now rely on the government to take care of the poor and elderly, a job previously entrusted to the church. In Deuteronomy God says in the "year of the tithe, you shall give it to the Levite, the alien, the fatherless and the widow". Through the entire scriptures (we'll even read tomorrow) the theme of caring for orphans and widows is repeated.

The book of James implores us to take action. It's time we stop sitting by and hearing a great sermon, then heading home, turning on the TV and wasting our lives.

If there is one thing this book should be able to tell you, it is that God can use anyone at any time to accomplish anything. What is it God is telling you to do? Don't sit around waiting for someone else, just do it!

Specific time spent with the Lord today and what was done:

_____

_____

Write out the memory verse for the week:

_____

_____

_____

_____

_____

In your own words, write about what the Lord is saying to you through the Verses for today:

_____

_____

_____

_____

_____

How do the Theme for the Day and/or Week apply to your life now?

_____

_____

_____

_____

_____

_____

WILLIAM JORDAN

As you were studying the word for today, what did you learn or discover?

_____

_____

_____

_____

_____

_____

Using the psalm you read today as a guide, write your own psalm to the Lord from your own heart:

_____

_____

_____

_____

_____

_____

_____

_____

_____

_____

_____

Prayer requests and/or prayers answered (share with your Father from your heart):

_____

_____

_____

_____

_____

_____

What else is the Lord putting on your heart today?

_____

_____

_____

_____

_____

_____

What other scriptures did you read today that were most impactful? How did they speak to you?

_____

_____

_____

_____

_____

Week #: **1**   Day #: **7**   Today's Date: _____

Chapter for the Week: **James 1**   Verses for today: **26-27**

Theme for the Week: **choice**

Theme for the Day: **bridle the tongue**

Word Study for Today: **bridle**   Psalm for Today: **Psalm 32**

How many friendships have been destroyed by a careless word or phrase? How much damage has been done by words used without thought, or in the heat of the moment. How many families there where one member will not speak to another because of something said that can't be taken back.

The tongue can be used for sharing the gospel, exhorting another brother in Christ. That same tongue can be used in an instant to wound someone deeply. You can use your tongue to speak blessing or cursing.

James speaks of bridling the tongue. A bridle is used to control a horse and make it go where you want it to. If you have ever ridden a horse and realized it didn't want to do what you were telling it to, it can be a very scary moment. With a bridle in its mouth, even the most uncontrollable horse can usually be brought to a halt in a short time.

Each of us needs to be able to put a bridle in our own mouth to control what comes out, especially in this day and age where every word has the chance to be recorded and replayed for generations. We must remember our own words can be used for us or against us, to bring glory to our God, or to damage the cause of Christ.

If you have spoken words you later regretted, stop to ask the Lord to provide an opportunity for you to repair the damage you have caused. Look for opportunities to slowly restore relationships that were broken due to words you desire to take back.

While you can't undo your words, you can begin to speak new life into people and situations. God can do all things.

Specific time spent with the Lord today and what was done:

_____

_____

Write out the memory verse for the week:

_____

_____

_____

_____

_____

In your own words, write about what the Lord is saying to you through the Verses for today:

_____

_____

_____

_____

_____

How do the Theme for the Day and/or Week apply to your life now?

_____

_____

_____

_____

_____

_____

_____

As you were studying the word for today, what did you learn or discover?

_____

_____

_____

_____

_____

_____

Using the psalm you read today as a guide, write your own psalm to the Lord from your own heart:

_____

_____

_____

_____

_____

_____

_____

_____

_____

_____

_____

Prayer requests and/or prayers answered (share with your Father from your heart):

_____

_____

_____

_____

_____

_____

What else is the Lord putting on your heart today?

_____

_____

_____

_____

_____

_____

What other scriptures did you read today that were most impactful? How did they speak to you?

_____

_____

_____

_____

_____

Five
A Tithe of Time, Week 2

You have made it through the first week!

Like any program of change, you've probably had some challenges this week. Hopefully the enthusiasm you started with and the excitement of drawing closer to God have carried you through the first week.

As you begin this second week, spend a little of your Tithe of Time reflecting on the goodness of the Lord. He loves you far beyond anything we can describe or even imagine. He desires a relationship with you that is more fulfilling than anything else you can ever experience.

The theme for week two is faith and works. In the second chapter of James, God will continue deepening your faith, and we will read what He expects of us related to our works here on earth.

For years, I lived my life as a Christian, loving and worshiping God. However, if you looked at my works, you could wonder where God was in them. I'm not saying I was backslidden or turning away from God, I worshiped God with my mouth, and tried to follow His commands. Yet what I did with the rest of my life was really based on what I enjoyed and what made me happy.

The Lord did not create me, or you, in a casual or abstract way. We were not formed by Him purposeless and for no meaning. God created you and me with a very specific intent. *He has a plan.*

The first step in our study in James was to focus on the theme of choice. We can choose to truly put God first in every area of our life, or only in most areas. To walk the path God has laid out for us, we must now deepen our faith, and let Him direct our path to the work He has prepared for us.

I refer to this throughout as the "great work" that God has placed in you. You may already be able to see it, or you may still be restoring a relationship with God that has grown distant over time. Either way, it should be humbling and thrilling to know God has His eye on you, and He has a plan. Our job is to walk in faith and humility, to allow Him to accomplish His plan in us.

Week #: **2**   Day #: **1**   Today's Date: _____

Chapter for the Week: **James 2**   Verses for today: **1-4**

Theme for the Week: **faith & works**

Theme for the Day: **partiality**

Word Study for Today: **partiality**   Psalm for Today: **Psalm 81**

Memory verse for the week: **James 2:14-18**

"You can't judge a book by its cover" is an age-old saying. Of course, another saying is, "you only have one chance to make a first impression."

Studies have shown people will decide within six seconds if they are going to like or dislike a person they meet. Talk about judging a book by its cover!

As Christians, are we guilty of judging people based on how they look, or speak, or the kind of car they drive? Face it, we live in a society that is infatuated with appearances. Even within our churches we find these kinds of visual judgments are being made.

When God examines a person, the Bible tells us He judges the heart. It doesn't matter to God if you have the latest fashions, technology toys or designer home décor. What matters to Him is that we are seeking first His kingdom and His righteousness, not seeking after the things of this world.

While we can't examine the heart as God can, the Lord does tell us those who follow Him will be known by their fruit. Are you judging people by their fruit, or by the window dressing based on their wealth?

Search your own heart. How is it that you want people to judge you? Have you fallen into the trap of using wealth or appearances to try and influence others?

Be careful you are not worrying about impressing other people with the things of this world. There's nothing wrong with wearing nice clothes, or driving a nice car. But if you do those things to win the approval of people, you probably need to ask God to help you refocus on your heart.

Specific time spent with the Lord today and what was done:

_____

_____

Write out the memory verse for the week:

_____

_____

_____

_____

_____

_____

_____

_____

_____

_____

In your own words, write about what the Lord is saying to you through the Verses for today:

_____

_____

_____

_____

_____

_____

_____

_____

How do the Theme for the Day and/or Week apply to your life now?

_____

_____

_____

_____

_____

_____

As you were studying the word for today, what did you learn or discover?

_____

_____

_____

_____

_____

_____

Using the psalm you read today as a guide, write your own psalm to the Lord from your own heart:

_____

_____

_____

_____

_____

_____

_____

_____

_____

_____

_____

Prayer requests and/or prayers answered (share with your Father from your heart):

_____

_____

_____

_____

_____

What else is the Lord putting on your heart today?

_____

_____

_____

_____

_____

_____

_____

What other scriptures did you read today that were most impactful? How did they speak to you?

_____

_____

_____

_____

_____

Week #: **2**   Day #: **2**   Today's Date: _____

Chapter for the Week: **James 2**   Verses for today: **5-7**

Theme for the Week: **faith & works**

Theme for the Day: **honor the poor**

Word Study for Today: **heirs**   Psalm for Today: **Psalm 105**

I live in Orange County, California, one of the wealthiest counties in the country. For my vocation, I run a financial planning firm, so even within one of the richest counties, I work with some of the richest people.

I see an interesting mix of people in my office ranging from one extreme or the other. Some have no compassion or heart for those who do not have the same earthly riches they have. Others are givers who truly honor those who do not have as much.

The Bible tells us the poor of this world should be honored by us, it is sin to look down on them due to their position. Still people make this mistake and judge others based on their bank account.

The Bible is filled with those who were poor, and who were loved of God. Jesus cherished the poor, and treated them exactly the same as everyone else. God doesn't care about the contents of our checking account, only the character of our heart.

Some of my financial planning clients dress extremely well, live in huge houses and have all the trappings you would expect. Others live in average houses, dress casual and in all ways act as if they don't have the kind of wealth they have. In my business, if I decided who to take on as a client based on first impression, I might miss a great person and client.

Far more significant than use in business, is the personal and spiritual application. Who knows if that brother in difficult financial circumstances wasn't put there by the Lord for you to minister to. What if God wants to bless you through that person in any number of ways? Always remember God judges the heart, and not the outward appearance. Learn to set aside the ways the world judges people, and focus on the heart.

Specific time spent with the Lord today and what was done:

_____

_____

Write out the memory verse for the week:

_____

_____

_____

_____

_____

_____

_____

_____

_____

In your own words, write about what the Lord is saying to you through the Verses for today:

_____

_____

_____

_____

_____

_____

_____

How do the Theme for the Day and/or Week apply to your life now?

_____

_____

_____

_____

_____

_____

_____

As you were studying the word for today, what did you learn or discover?

_____

_____

_____

_____

_____

_____

_____

Using the psalm you read today as a guide, write your own psalm to the Lord from your own heart:

_____

_____

_____

_____

_____

_____

_____

_____

_____

_____

_____

Prayer requests and/or prayers answered (share with your Father from your heart):

_____

_____

_____

_____

_____

What else is the Lord putting on your heart today?

_____

_____

_____

_____

_____

_____

_____

What other scriptures did you read today that were most impactful? How did they speak to you?

_____

_____

_____

_____

_____

Week #: **2**   Day #: **3**   Today's Date: _____

Chapter for the Week: **James 2**   Verses for today: **8-10**

Theme for the Week: **faith & works**

Theme for the Day: **love your neighbor**

Word Study for Today: **neighbor**   Psalm for Today: **Psalm 101**

In Luke 10, Jesus is asked to clarify the scriptural mandate to "love your neighbor as yourself". When questioned about who our neighbor really is, Jesus answers with the parable of the good Samaritan.

Remember at this time, the Jews looked down on the Samaritans, so a Samaritan would have no reason at all to go out of his way to try and bless the Jews or do good things for them.

Imagine you are walking down the road, and come upon someone who has wronged you. They have ridiculed you, put you down in front of other people and generally treated you poorly, even though you have never done anything to them.

You find them lying on the ground clearly hurt. How many of us would have to try and beat back that first fleshly instinct to think this person had it coming to them, that God had taken revenge for us.

Instead, Jesus tells us our neighbor is this person lying there. Not only is God going to call on us to set aside our own feelings, we are actually expected to go far out of our way to help this person.

I don't know about you, but this feels like God is going a bit too far. And yet that is exactly what Jesus would have us do. In fact, He did it for us.

We are all guilty of rejecting Jesus. The Bible is clear "all have sinned and fallen short of the glory of God" Romans 3:23. Yet in our state of depravity, Jesus laid down His life for us. So I ask you, if our savior can die for us when we didn't deserve it, can we find it in our hearts to love our neighbor, one of His children, as ourselves?

Specific time spent with the Lord today and what was done:

_____

_____

Write out the memory verse for the week:

_____

_____

_____

_____

_____

_____

_____

_____

_____

In your own words, write about what the Lord is saying to you through the Verses for today:

_____

_____

_____

_____

_____

_____

_____

_____

How do the Theme for the Day and/or Week apply to your life now?

_____

_____

_____

_____

_____

_____

_____

As you were studying the word for today, what did you learn or discover?

_____

_____

_____

_____

_____

_____

_____

Using the psalm you read today as a guide, write your own psalm to the Lord from your own heart:

_____

_____

_____

_____

_____

_____

_____

_____

_____

_____

_____

_____

Prayer requests and/or prayers answered (share with your Father from your heart):

_____

_____

_____

_____

_____

_____

What else is the Lord putting on your heart today?

_____

_____

_____

_____

_____

_____

_____

What other scriptures did you read today that were most impactful? How did they speak to you?

_____

_____

_____

_____

_____

Week #: **2**   Day #: **4**   Today's Date: _____

Chapter for the Week: **James 2**   Verses for today: **11-13**

Theme for the Week: **faith & works**   Theme for the Day: **the law**

Word Study for Today: **mercy**   Psalm for Today: **Psalm 28**

I once read in a book on the psychology of birth order. Firstborn children grow up wanting justice while the lastborn children are more apt to want mercy. As a firstborn, I can identify with this sense of justice. As a father, I hear "that's not fair" often coming from my eldest!

Beginning in Matthew 18:21, Jesus gave us the parable of the unmerciful servant. The servant's master forgave a huge amount of money, ten thousand talents. Then the servant went out and had another servant thrown in jail for not repaying a hundred denarii, which was very little.

When the master heard of this, he had the servant thrown in jail to be tortured until he could repay all he owed. Jesus tells us our heavenly Father will likewise judge us unless we forgive our brother.

It's almost ironic that when we are dealing with others, we tend to judge with a harsher standard than the one we would choose to have applied to ourselves. When the shoe is on the other foot, we ask for mercy.

Face it, others are going to blow it. Whether they are sinning against us, or just make a mistake that ends up hurting us. If we spend our whole lives demanding justice every time someone offends us, we will most likely drive ourselves crazy.

I've often seen this happen in churches. It could be a pastor, a lay leader or a Christian brother/sister who does something that hurts someone else, and the next thing you know, people are upset, talking to other people and even going so far as to the church.

If we could only learn mercy triumphs over judgment! Remember all have sinned, including you and me. Don't hesitate to give mercy!

Specific time spent with the Lord today and what was done:

_____

_____

71

Write out the memory verse for the week:

_____

_____

_____

_____

_____

_____

_____

_____

In your own words, write about what the Lord is saying to you through the Verses for today:

_____

_____

_____

_____

_____

_____

_____

_____

How do the Theme for the Day and/or Week apply to your life now?

_____

_____

_____

_____

_____

_____

As you were studying the word for today, what did you learn or discover?

_____

_____

_____

_____

_____

_____

Using the psalm you read today as a guide, write your own psalm to the Lord from your own heart:

_____

_____

_____

_____

_____

_____

_____

_____

_____

_____

_____

Prayer requests and/or prayers answered (share with your Father from your heart):

_____

_____

_____

_____

_____

What else is the Lord putting on your heart today?

_____

_____

_____

_____

_____

_____

_____

What other scriptures did you read today that were most impactful? How did they speak to you?

_____

_____

_____

_____

_____

Week #: **2**   Day #: **5**   Today's Date: _____

Chapter for the Week: **James 2**   Verses for today: **14-17**

Theme for the Week: **faith & works**

Theme for the Day: **faith without works**

Word Study for Today: **faith**   Psalm for Today: **Psalm 146**

I find it amazing that the word *faith* appears only twice in the King James version of the Old Testament; however, the New Testament reveals two hundred and twenty nine appearances of the same word. Interesting.

In my childhood, I learned Hebrews 11:6; "Without faith, it is impossible to please God". Clearly we all want to have the kind of faith that will please God. When I read about faith in the Bible, I read about a complete and unwavering conviction that something is true, regardless of the situation or the facts as they may seem.

It's the same faith spoken of moving mountains, the same faith Jesus says healed the paralytic in Matthew 9:2, and made the woman well later in that same chapter. To borrow a slogan, this is not your grandfather's faith!

This faith is alive and active, a faith that brings about God's will on this earth. Jesus is repeatedly showing us our faith moves God, and without faith we cannot please Him. No wonder James tells us "faith without works is dead"!

We are called to have faith in order to please God. Jesus tells us our faith can make us well, move mountains and perform miracles. God says through James that if we have faith we will have works as our fruit. Our works demonstrate and prove our faith. This seems a clear progression.

God is calling each of us to exercise our faith, to strengthen and grow it. "Faith comes by hearing, and hearing by the Word of God." Romans 10:17. This time you have been spending with God is building your faith. Ask God to give you an opportunity to let your works match your faith.

Specific time spent with the Lord today and what was done:

_____

_____

Write out the memory verse for the week:

_____

_____

_____

_____

_____

_____

_____

_____

_____

_____

In your own words, write about what the Lord is saying to you through the Verses for today:

_____

_____

_____

_____

_____

_____

_____

_____

WILLIAM JORDAN

How do the Theme for the Day and/or Week apply to your life now?

_____

_____

_____

_____

_____

As you were studying the word for today, what did you learn or discover?

_____

_____

_____

_____

_____

_____

Using the psalm you read today as a guide, write your own psalm to the Lord from your own heart:

_____

_____

_____

_____

_____

_____

_____

_____

_____

_____

_____

_____

Prayer requests and/or prayers answered (share with your Father from your heart):

_____

_____

_____

_____

_____

_____

What else is the Lord putting on your heart today?

_____

_____

_____

_____

_____

_____

_____

_____

What other scriptures did you read today that were most impactful? How did they speak to you?

_____

_____

_____

_____

_____

Week #: **2**   Day #: **6**   Today's Date: _____

Chapter for the Week: **James 2**   Verses for today: **18-20**

Theme for the Week: **faith & works**

Theme for the Day: **faith without works**

Word Study for Today: **works**   Psalm for Today: **Psalm 9**

When I was a young man going through some very difficult financial times, I shared my needs with a dear pastor. This man of God shared with me and encouraged me, and when I went to leave, he placed $40 in my hand. It was money he didn't have, but it was his faith in action.

I knew how little he had at the time, so I tried to refuse the money. He wouldn't take it back and told me I had to keep it because it was "sacred" money. God bless him! This Pastor was working out his faith.

As my wife and I have grown, in our lives and our faith, God has given us opportunities to let our works match our faith. I don't want to share specific details, because we've laid those treasures up in heaven.

I can say in general, there have been many times we have been called on, as my pastor was, to give what we didn't have. Or sometimes to give what we did have, but thought we would use for other purposes.

The works that demonstrate your faith don't have to be financial. I know people who have taken someone into their home and let them live with them. God will bless you for this!

I know another couple who continually press on in a specific area of ministry for the Lord, even though they would really like to step down from the responsibilities they have been given. However God has called them to live out their faith with works in this area.

The good news is you don't have to merely hope God will give you an opportunity to live by faith, and let your works prove that faith. Rest assured God will give you opportunities, daily in most cases, to live out that faith. Even today God will open a door for you. Be ready!

Specific time spent with the Lord today and what was done:

_____

_____

Write out the memory verse for the week:

_____

_____

_____

_____

_____

_____

_____

_____

In your own words, write about what the Lord is saying to you through the Verses for today:

_____

_____

_____

_____

_____

_____

_____

How do the Theme for the Day and/or Week apply to your life now?

_____

_____

_____

_____

_____

_____

_____

As you were studying the word for today, what did you learn or discover?

_____

_____

_____

_____

_____

_____

_____

Using the psalm you read today as a guide, write your own psalm to the Lord from your own heart:

_____

_____

_____

_____

_____

_____

_____

_____

_____

_____

_____

Prayer requests and/or prayers answered (share with your Father from your heart):

_____

_____

_____

_____

_____

What else is the Lord putting on your heart today?

_____

_____

_____

_____

_____

_____

_____

What other scriptures did you read today that were most impactful? How did they speak to you?

_____

_____

_____

_____

_____

Week #: **2**   Day #: **7**   Today's Date: _____

Chapter for the Week: **James 2**   Verses for today: **21-26**

Theme for the Week: **faith & works**

Theme for the Day: **justified by works**

Word Study for Today: **justified**   Psalm for Today: **Psalm 51**

Some Christians get nervous with using the word faith, because it brings up visions of someone having "faith" for a new fancy car, or a big fat bank account. The concept of faith can be taken to an extreme and some can fall into the trap of treating God like a living version of Aladdin's magic lamp.

For others, they think of faith as a silent, boring and weary acceptance God is in charge of their lives. It is like fate and doesn't mean anything. They know He's there, and figure their faith is covered by that knowledge.

Here we are in James, in one of those sections that can be taken out of context and used to build another false view of faith. One can try to take these few verses from James, and build a false theology that we can somehow earn our way into heaven through our works.

We must view all of scripture in its totality, and not allow any one verse to take on more weight than it should. The whole of scripture clearly and completely states that without the work of Jesus Christ on the cross, we are lost. The only way to heaven is through Jesus and acceptance of His death as a sacrifice for our sins.

I don't want to get into a major theological debate on the subject of this verse. In knowing that accepting Jesus as Lord is the only way to heaven, I can then accept that in some way other than salvation, our works justify us. Just as the Biblical principal of water baptism does not save us. For if it did, how could the thief on the cross be promised salvation by Jesus.

The lesson of today's reading is we must submit all interpretations of scripture to the Lord. We must judge every word and thought in the light of His entire word, for only His word is truth.

Specific time spent with the Lord today and what was done:

_____

_____

Write out the memory verse for the week:

In your own words, write about what the Lord is saying to you through the Verses for today:

How do the Theme for the Day and/or Week apply to your life now?

_____

_____

_____

_____

_____

As you were studying the word for today, what did you learn or discover?

_____

_____

_____

_____

_____

_____

Using the psalm you read today as a guide, write your own psalm to the Lord from your own heart:

_____

_____

_____

_____

_____

_____

_____

_____

_____

_____

_____

_____

Prayer requests and/or prayers answered (share with your Father from your heart):

_____

_____

_____

_____

_____

_____

What else is the Lord putting on your heart today?

_____

_____

_____

_____

_____

_____

_____

_____

What other scriptures did you read today that were most impactful? How did they speak to you?

_____

_____

_____

_____

_____

Six
A Tithe of Time, Week Three

We're two weeks in! I know you have been making sacrifices in how you spend your time, and you've probably had some moments where you were tempted to reverse course. Stand fast! Focus on the ways your faith has already been increased, and the strong sense God's presence that you are experiencing.

Last week we focused on the theme of our faith and our works. This week we turn our attention to the practice of peace.

I find the theme of peace to be so appropriate for this study, especially as we approach the middle of the forty days. A Tithe of Time is about peace, being still, and listening for the still, small voice of God that speaks to you below the roar of the busy day.

Many Christians have lost their peace. They worry and fret, stress out and freak out. This shouldn't be. It's not hard to understand why though, without your Father's calm, strong voice to reassure you, life can seem to be so out of control.

Sometimes my children hurt themselves. They fall and scrape a knee, or bang into something. Most times all they need is for me to hold them and tell them they are okay. Intuitively we know God is in control and we don't need to worry, but sometimes we just need to feel His presence and hear Him tell us everything is okay.

A few years back I went through some rather terrible business times. Many people asked me how I could be doing so well with the things that were going on. I really couldn't explain it. I can only say that in the midst of the tempest, when I should have been burning with anger or shaking with fear, I had a deep and abiding peace. That is the "peace of God which passes all understanding"! (Philippians 4:7)

I deeply and sincerely hope you are beginning to experience this kind of peace. It is divine peace. There is only one source. Amazingly, you and I have access to that source, our Lord and Savior Jesus Christ.

Week #: **3**   Day #: **1**   Today's Date: _____

Chapter for the Week: **James 3**   Verses for today: **1-2**

Theme for the Week: **peace**

Theme for the Day: **stricter judgment**

Word Study for Today: **teacher**   Psalm for Today: **Psalm 25**

Memory verse for the week: **James 3:17-18**

I'll always remember the comment I heard from a pastor when discussing how you can know if you are called to be a pastor. He said first, ask yourself this question: If you knew right now you could never be a pastor, what else would you consider doing?

After a few moments he made his point. He said if you had any answer to that question other than "there's nothing else I could do except be a pastor", then you better go do that other thing you were considering.

Being a pastor or teacher is not something to be taken lightly. It can lead to tremendous opportunities to advance the kingdom of God. At the same time, there is no other area of work in which a person can do so much damage to the cause of Christ.

Think of pastors and teachers who have stumbled on the national stage in our country. How much damage has been done to the church, and to our nation? Here in James, as in other areas of scripture, teachers are warned they will be held to a stricter judgment.

We all will fall short from time to time. But imagine this. When you sin, and need to repent, what if you had to stand in front of hundreds of people who all look up to you, and tell them of your failings? It's hard enough to confess our sins to each other, but how about to a whole congregation?

I have personally seen less mature Christians drawn away from the church and their faith weakened because a leader they looked up to and respected sinned. So the next time you must repent of a sin and confess it to someone, be thankful you are not a teacher. And remember to pray for them!

Specific time spent with the Lord today and what was done:

_____

_____

Write out the memory verse for the week:

_____

_____

_____

_____

_____

In your own words, write about what the Lord is saying to you through the Verses for today:

_____

_____

_____

_____

_____

How do the Theme for the Day and/or Week apply to your life now?

_____

_____

_____

_____

_____

_____

As you were studying the word for today, what did you learn or discover?

_____

_____

_____

_____

_____

_____

Using the psalm you read today as a guide, write your own psalm to the Lord from your own heart:

_____

_____

_____

_____

_____

_____

_____

_____

_____

_____

_____

_____

Prayer requests and/or prayers answered (share with your Father from your heart):

_____

_____

_____

_____

_____

What else is the Lord putting on your heart today?

_____

_____

_____

_____

_____

_____

What other scriptures did you read today that were most impactful? How did they speak to you?

_____

_____

_____

_____

_____

Week #: **3**   Day #: **2**   Today's Date: _____

Chapter for the Week: **James 3**   Verses for today: **3-5**

Theme for the Week: **peace**   Theme for the Day: **the tongue**

Word Study for Today: **tongue**   Psalm for Today: **Psalm 12**

God has a lot to say about our tongue. It's one of the reoccurring themes in the book of James. He continually warns us of the damage we can do if we are not careful to control it.

Several years ago, I had an exchange with another Christian that I still recall with regret. He had ostensibly come to me for some advice and counsel. We had attended the same church for years, and he had a good reputation and was well liked.

Unfortunately, our chat ended up taking place on one of those really horrible days when you aren't even close to your best. The day started with my wife and me having a huge fight about something I can't recall.

My day went from bad to worse and by the time this Christian brother showed up I was having a terrible day. My spirit was raw from the fight with my wife when I sat down to what I thought was a brief and pleasant conversation between Christian brothers.

This Christian man whom I had respected, launched into an unmerited verbal attack questioning me in many areas, even my integrity. He resisted every attempt at rational conversation even though his wife tried several times to salvage the conversation. After about 15 minutes I snapped at him that the conversation was over and said "I thought we were all Christians here".

It would take too long to list the damage I did with those words. No matter how justified I was in my anger at that moment, I crossed the line into sin. While I'd like to blame this other person and his lack of control over his tongue, I had the choice to keep silent, stand up and just walk out.

Learn to control your tongue.

Specific time spent with the Lord today and what was done:

_____

_____

Write out the memory verse for the week:

_____

_____

_____

_____

_____

_____

In your own words, write about what the Lord is saying to you through the Verses for today:

_____

_____

_____

_____

_____

_____

How do the Theme for the Day and/or Week apply to your life now?

_____

_____

_____

_____

_____

_____

As you were studying the word for today, what did you learn or discover?

_____

_____

_____

_____

_____

_____

Using the psalm you read today as a guide, write your own psalm to the Lord from your own heart:

_____

_____

_____

_____

_____

_____

_____

_____

_____

_____

Prayer requests and/or prayers answered (share with your Father from your heart):

_____

_____

_____

_____

_____

What else is the Lord putting on your heart today?

_____

_____

_____

_____

_____

_____

What other scriptures did you read today that were most impactful? How did they speak to you?

_____

_____

_____

_____

_____

Week #: **3**   Day #: **3**   Today's Date: _____

Chapter for the Week: **James 3**   Verses for today: **6-8**

Theme for the Week: **peace**   Theme for the Day: **tame the tongue**

Word Study for Today: **tame**   Psalm for Today: **Psalm 15**

In yesterday's discussion, I shared one careless moment when I lost control of my tongue. This sin hurt me and my walk with the Lord. I know my words also wounded this Christian man, whom I had respected.

Even worse, it caused this man to stumble in his walk with Christ. I tried to contact him to apologize and restore, but he had hardened his heart toward me. He refused to return my phone call, saying through a mutual acquaintance that he didn't want to "pursue the apology".

I can't say I have all the blame for this. As a Christian almost twenty years my senior, this man is accountable to the Lord for his own actions. However it grieves me to know that in some way, my moment of losing control of my tongue contributed to this. Clearly it did.

If this wasn't such a significant issue, the Lord would not have devoted so large a portion of the book of James to this topic. God knows that I'm not the only person who can lose control of my tongue.

You might wonder why this other Christian didn't apologize to me for his behavior. I think it's significant to realize his choice is totally beside the point. I am not responsible to the Lord for how someone else behaves, but I am accountable for what I choose in response. Too often we as Christians justify our behavior by excusing our sin because someone else sinned against us. That thought process is simply not biblical.

I did grow from this experience. I learned to recognize when I am having 'one of those days' where it is harder to maintain control over my tongue. I learned to stop talking when I feel righteous anger turning the corner towards sin, and to return a harsh word with a kind one. My I be fully prepared to follow God's perfect path when faced with this situation again.

Specific time spent with the Lord today and what was done:

_____

_____

Write out the memory verse for the week:

_____

_____

_____

_____

_____

In your own words, write about what the Lord is saying to you through the Verses for today:

_____

_____

_____

_____

_____

_____

How do the Theme for the Day and/or Week apply to your life now?

_____

_____

_____

_____

_____

_____

As you were studying the word for today, what did you learn or discover?

_____

_____

_____

_____

_____

_____

_____

Using the psalm you read today as a guide, write your own psalm to the Lord from your own heart:

_____

_____

_____

_____

_____

_____

_____

_____

_____

_____

_____

_____

Prayer requests and/or prayers answered (share with your Father from your heart):

_____

_____

_____

_____

_____

What else is the Lord putting on your heart today?

_____

_____

_____

_____

_____

What other scriptures did you read today that were most impactful? How did they speak to you?

_____

_____

_____

_____

_____

Week #: **3**   Day #: **4**   Today's Date: _____

Chapter for the Week: **James 3**   Verses for today: **9-10**

Theme for the Week: **peace**   Theme for the Day: **God's likeness**

Word Study for Today: **blessing**   Psalm for Today: **Psalm 24**

In our reading today, we will see that James continues to discuss the tongue by sharing how it can be used for both blessing and cursing. We've seen clearly how it can cause damage, now let me share with you a way it can be used for blessing.

My dear friend Scott Meacham is a Biblical Christian Psychologist who has developed a number of amazing communication tools. His success in helping couples restore marriages borders on the miraculous. He is the man I consider to be my spiritual father.

One tool he taught me is a Biblical anger tool. It's about forgiveness. It's really for the one forgiving, not the one being forgiven. Often, the person who needs to be forgiven doesn't want to be, or doesn't agree they even did anything wrong. We end up carrying around anger and resentment that can never be reconciled.

Scott taught me to have my own little "chat" with the person, when they aren't around. I usually do this while driving, or sometimes while taking a shower. Speak to the person as if they were there, and start by blessing them. Here is a model of Scott's script:

"William (address them by name). You are created by God in His image. He loves you and I can love the essence of you that is created in the image of God. And (always use the word "and", never "but") ... and I am angry with you because" and then share what your anger is about.

End with "This is one of the sins for which Jesus hung on the cross and died. I forgive you just as God, for Christ's sake, has also forgiven me. You may have to do this several times (for the same offence), but it has never failed to help me release anger that was only hurting me.

Specific time spent with the Lord today and what was done:

_____

_____

Write out the memory verse for the week:

_____

_____

_____

_____

_____

_____

In your own words, write about what the Lord is saying to you through the Verses for today:

_____

_____

_____

_____

_____

_____

How do the Theme for the Day and/or Week apply to your life now?

_____

_____

_____

_____

_____

_____

As you were studying the word for today, what did you learn or discover?

_____

_____

_____

_____

_____

_____

_____

Using the psalm you read today as a guide, write your own psalm to the Lord from your own heart:

_____

_____

_____

_____

_____

_____

_____

_____

_____

_____

_____

_____

Prayer requests and/or prayers answered (share with your Father from your heart):

_____

_____

_____

_____

_____

What else is the Lord putting on your heart today?

_____

_____

_____

_____

_____

What other scriptures did you read today that were most impactful? How did they speak to you?

_____

_____

_____

_____

_____

Week #: **3**   Day #: **5**   Today's Date: _____

Chapter for the Week: **James 3**   Verses for today: **11-12**

Theme for the Week: **peace**   Theme for the Day: **bear fruit**

Word Study for Today: **fruit**   Psalm for Today: **Psalm 104**

"By their fruit you will know them" (Matthew 7:16). In James, Matthew, and elsewhere in the Bible, Jesus tells us we can know the inward condition of people by looking at their fruit.

Most people who look at a tree cannot immediately tell you what kind of fruit it will produce. If you watch a tree long enough, in its season you will see the fruit it produces and discern what kind of tree it is.

Likewise, believers should bear good fruit as evidence of their relationship with the Lord. At the same time, those who come among the church who look so good on the outside at first, will eventually produce fruit after the kind of tree they are. With some people it becomes obvious more quickly, while with others it takes more time.

In that same section of Matthew, Jesus tells us not everyone who says to Him "Lord, Lord" will enter the kingdom of heaven. So it is not enough to know the right words and how to say them. Jesus goes on to say some will claim they prophesied in His name or cast out demons and performed miracles.

Even miracles are not to be used as a discernment someone's fruit. Instead, examine their life and how it has been changed due to their relationship with the Lord, and look for the fruit of those they have helped come to know the Lord.

Studies have shown most Christians never bring another person to Christ. Yet this is the command Jesus left us with at the end of the gospels, to share the gospel. Who do you need to talk to about Christ. Ask God to give you open doors to share your faith.

Specific time spent with the Lord today and what was done:

_____

_____

Write out the memory verse for the week:

_____

_____

_____

_____

_____

_____

In your own words, write about what the Lord is saying to you through the Verses for today:

_____

_____

_____

_____

_____

_____

How do the Theme for the Day and/or Week apply to your life now?

_____

_____

_____

_____

_____

_____

As you were studying the word for today, what did you learn or discover?

_____

_____

_____

_____

_____

_____

Using the psalm you read today as a guide, write your own psalm to the Lord from your own heart:

_____

_____

_____

_____

_____

_____

_____

_____

_____

_____

_____

Prayer requests and/or prayers answered (share with your Father from your heart):

_____

_____

_____

_____

_____

What else is the Lord putting on your heart today?

_____

_____

_____

_____

_____

_____

What other scriptures did you read today that were most impactful? How did they speak to you?

_____

_____

_____

_____

_____

Week #: **3**   Day #: **6**   Today's Date: _____

Chapter for the Week: **James 3**   Verses for today: **13-16**

Theme for the Week: **peace**

Theme for the Day: **meekness of wisdom**

Word Study for Today: **wisdom**   Psalm for Today: **Psalm 111**

When I read the phrase the "meekness of wisdom", I can't help but again mention my dear brother Scott Meacham. Someone who knows both of us joked once that even his name is pronounced "meek-um". If there is ever a person who embodies meekness, it is Scott.

This scripture speaks to me of Scott. The Lord says in James that anyone who is wise and understanding will show it, by their behavior and deeds, in the meekness of wisdom.

"The fear of the Lord is the beginning of wisdom" is shared throughout the Proverbs. If someone has wisdom and the fear of the Lord, it is easy to see how they can be meek in wisdom. A healthy fear of the Lord helps us recognize instantly that wisdom truly comes from God. We are just the vessel, and the originator is the Lord.

On the opposite side of the spectrum from wisdom and the fear of the Lord is jealousy, pride and selfish ambition. I saw this first hand in a situation with a Christian brother who used to work with me.

Over time what looked like wisdom clearly turned into selfish ambition. Wisdom will not strive with this kind of ambition. This man's wisdom departed as his selfishness took control. James 3:16 says, out of selfish ambition comes disorder, and every evil thing.

No one intends to fall prey to selfish ambition or jealousy. If we do not continually submit ourselves to God's will and maintain our fear of the Lord, the enemy will step in and sow the seeds of those sins. In time, our untended garden can become overgrown with the weeds of pride, jealousy and selfishness. Be vigilant to watch for these things in your life and pray the Holy Spirit would constantly renew your fear of the Lord.

Specific time spent with the Lord today and what was done:

_____

_____

Write out the memory verse for the week:

_____

_____

_____

_____

_____

In your own words, write about what the Lord is saying to you through the Verses for today:

_____

_____

_____

_____

_____

_____

How do the Theme for the Day and/or Week apply to your life now?

_____

_____

_____

_____

_____

_____

As you were studying the word for today, what did you learn or discover?

_____

_____

_____

_____

_____

_____

Using the psalm you read today as a guide, write your own psalm to the Lord from your own heart:

_____

_____

_____

_____

_____

_____

_____

_____

_____

Prayer requests and/or prayers answered (share with your Father from your heart):

_____

_____

_____

_____

_____

What else is the Lord putting on your heart today?

_____

_____

_____

_____

_____

What other scriptures did you read today that were most impactful? How did they speak to you?

_____

_____

_____

_____

_____

Week #: **3**   Day #: **7**   Today's Date: _____

Chapter for the Week: **James 3**   Verses for today: **17-18**

Theme for the Week: **peace**

Theme for the Day: **wisdom is from above**

Word Study for Today: **peace**   Psalm for Today: **Psalm 37**

Early in the book of James, we read that if anyone lacks wisdom they should ask of God who "gives generously to all without finding fault".

God wants us to have wisdom. He offers it to us and gives us His word to gain wisdom and to develop a healthy fear of the Lord. You can ask the Lord for wisdom in faith, just as discussed throughout James.

James 3:17 describes divine wisdom by saying, "The wisdom from above is first pure, then peaceable, gentle, reasonable, full of mercy and good fruits, unwavering without hypocrisy." When you see this kind of wisdom in someone, you can trust it comes from the Lord.

God greatly desires to give us wisdom, the entire book of Proverbs is placed in the Bible. God's wisdom is placed throughout the Bible, to be planted like a seed in our spirit.

In Second Chronicles, the Lord comes to Solomon and suggests he ask whatever he wants from God. Of all the things Solomon could have asked for, he asks the Lord for wisdom. God is so pleased by this He gives Solomon not only wisdom but also "wealth, riches and honor" beyond what any king has ever experienced.

God is pleased when you ask for wisdom. Proverbs 2:6 says "the Lord gives wisdom" and Proverbs 3:13 says "blessed is the man who finds wisdom". In Proverbs 4:7 the Lord says "get wisdom, though it cost you all you have". It is our job to seek for and pursue wisdom, and it is up to the Lord to grant wisdom.

Take time today to pray for wisdom. Seek it with all your heart.

Specific time spent with the Lord today and what was done:

_____

_____

Write out the memory verse for the week:

_____

_____

_____

_____

_____

In your own words, write about what the Lord is saying to you through the Verses for today:

_____

_____

_____

_____

_____

_____

How do the Theme for the Day and/or Week apply to your life now?

_____

_____

_____

_____

_____

_____

As you were studying the word for today, what did you learn or discover?

_____

_____

_____

_____

_____

_____

Using the psalm you read today as a guide, write your own psalm to the Lord from your own heart:

_____

_____

_____

_____

_____

_____

_____

_____

_____

_____

_____

Prayer requests and/or prayers answered (share with your Father from your heart):

_____

_____

_____

_____

_____

What else is the Lord putting on your heart today?

_____

_____

_____

_____

_____

_____

What other scriptures did you read today that were most impactful? How did they speak to you?

_____

_____

_____

_____

_____

Seven
A Tithe of Time, Week Four

Believe it or not, we've passed the halfway point of our Tithe of Time. We are beginning the fourth week.

As we continue with our study, I want to remind you that our study in James is meant to be a guide and a process to get you going, not the sum total of your time with the Lord.

You should be using the Theme for the Day and Week, along with the word study for the day, to help guide you to other areas of study. This is meant to be a help, but not a limitation.

If, in the middle of the day or week, you sense the Lord leading you to different areas of the Bible, different word studies or different verses to meditate on, go with His plan! You can always return to where you left off a few days or even weeks later.

This book is a tool. Use it to help direct you, but don't be restricted by it. You may find that God speaks to you in different ways or takes you in different directions. This is wonderful. Learn to listen for God's voice and His leading in all that you do.

This study is a good place to practice listening to God, and hearing His voice. As you develop this and become more accustomed to the Lord's voice, you will be able to hear Him speak to you more and more each day!

At the beginning of the fourth week, you should already know you are changing. God has been speaking to you through this process, and if you have been faithful to give Him your tithe of time each day, then you are drawing near to Him.

Isaiah 55:11 says His word "shall not return void". So as you draw near to Him, I know He will be faithful to draw near to you. We'll read about this more specifically in a few days.

So far in James, we've spent time on the themes of choice, our faith and our works, and last week on peace. In James 4, we turn our thoughts towards humility.

Week #: **4**   Day #: **1**   Today's Date: _____

Chapter for the Week: **James 4**   Verses for today: **1-2**

Theme for the Week: **humility**

Theme for the Day: **wars and fights**

Word Study for Today: **lust**   Psalm for Today: **Psalm 78**

Memory verse for the week: **James 4:6-8**

God is talking to us about our quarrels and our fights. Where do these things come from?

Humility can be one of the most challenging characteristics to study or practice. Just try telling someone "I'm working on humility". It almost sounds prideful to even say, not to mention that humility is the opposite of pride, which was the original sin.

God desires for us to be humble. He sent His only Son, Jesus, to model what humility looks like in the flesh.

These verses explain that conflict comes from the lusts and desires from within us. On a global scale, you could rightly say every war in history has been waged for some fleshly desire. Whether it is from desire for wealth, power, fame or some other desire, all wars have been started for the same reasons.

Isn't it true concerning the fights between us? God says it is. It is our internal desires, our lusts. We are caught up inside this fleshly body that was born into sin, bound to our sin nature. Even Paul says in Romans 7:15 "I am doing the very thing I hate".

So it's not a surprise that we all fall prey to our flesh and to its desires. Thankfully we have the Holy Spirit inside of us to direct us and guide us. We need to lean on the Holy Spirit daily, moment by moment.

The Christian journey is not to see how much we can accomplish in our own flesh. It is an opportunity to daily walk in the spirit and lean entirely on Him. 1 John 4:4 says, "Greater is He who is in us than he who is in the world"!

Specific time spent with the Lord today and what was done:

_____

_____

Write out the memory verse for the week:

_____

_____

_____

_____

_____

_____

_____

In your own words, write about what the Lord is saying to you through the Verses for today:

_____

_____

_____

_____

_____

_____

How do the Theme for the Day and/or Week apply to your life now?

_____

_____

_____

_____

_____

_____

_____

As you were studying the word for today, what did you learn or discover?

_____

_____

_____

_____

_____

_____

Using the psalm you read today as a guide, write your own psalm to the Lord from your own heart:

_____

_____

_____

_____

_____

_____

_____

_____

_____

_____

_____

_____

_____

Prayer requests and/or prayers answered (share with your Father from your heart):

_____

_____

_____

_____

_____

_____

What else is the Lord putting on your heart today?

_____

_____

_____

_____

_____

_____

_____

What other scriptures did you read today that were most impactful?
How did they speak to you?

_____

_____

_____

_____

_____

Week #: **4**   Day #: **2**   Today's Date: _____

Chapter for the Week: **James 4**   Verses for today: **3-5**

Theme for the Week: **humility**

Theme for the Day: **you ask amiss**

Word Study for Today: **world**   Psalm for Today: **Psalm 22**

Here is another verse often taken out of context. James says you "do not have because you do not ask God". Unfortunately, this verse is pulled out when someone wants something and they want God to deliver it. It just doesn't work that way.

Let's consider the actual context of what God is saying. He does say that we do not have because we do not ask. However God knew that we might try to use this verse incorrectly, so He immediately gives us the context in verse 3. "You ask and do not receive, because you ask amiss, that you may spend it on your pleasures."

Just when we are feeling all puffed up and holy, God hits us squarely in the head with the truth. We ask and do not receive because what we ask for is coming from our fleshly desires and our sin nature.

This world is tempting in many different ways. There is something about this world that can appeal to everyone. It's like going to Disneyland. Whatever type of ride or entertainment you want, you can probably find it there.

The problem is we run the risk of falling in love with the world. There's a reason the Bible tells us in Matthew 6:20 to "store up for yourself treasures in heaven". If we get so caught up and focused on the things of this world we have our treasures stored here, then it's no surprise when we fall in love with this world.

I refer to this life as "the waiting room". We have an appointment to see the King. Anticipating what follows this life should leave us breathless with anticipation. This world is like the few minutes spent in a waiting room anxiously waiting to see Him face to face!

Specific time spent with the Lord today and what was done:

_____

_____

Write out the memory verse for the week:

_____

_____

_____

_____

_____

_____

_____

In your own words, write about what the Lord is saying to you through the Verses for today:

_____

_____

_____

_____

_____

How do the Theme for the Day and/or Week apply to your life now?

_____

_____

_____

_____

_____

_____

_____

_____

_____

As you were studying the word for today, what did you learn or discover?

_____

_____

_____

_____

_____

_____

Using the psalm you read today as a guide, write your own psalm to the Lord from your own heart:

_____

_____

_____

_____

_____

_____

_____

_____

_____

_____

_____

Prayer requests and/or prayers answered (share with your Father from your heart):

_____

_____

_____

_____

_____

What else is the Lord putting on your heart today?

_____

_____

_____

_____

_____

_____

What other scriptures did you read today that were most impactful? How did they speak to you?

_____

_____

_____

_____

_____

Week #: 4   Day #: **3**   Today's Date: _____

Chapter for the Week: **James 4**   Verses for today: **6**

Theme for the Week: **humility**

Theme for the Day: **God opposes the proud**

Word Study for Today: **grace**   Psalm for Today: **Psalm 84**

This has become my life verse. About five years ago, at a men's retreat, this verse shook me like thunder. "God opposes the proud but gives grace to the humble." At the time I didn't realize it appears several times in scripture, so imagine my surprise when the same verse kept popping up in front of my face.

I can be a little slow at times, but when God keeps hitting me over the head with the same verse, eventually even I catch on that He might be trying to tell me something.

God was telling me I was proud. That I thought I could make it on my own with my own strength. As you already know, I was wrong on an epic scale.

Seven years into my marriage, I found myself sitting in a car in the rain wondering why God had cursed me. I have never considered divorce as an option, so I poured out my spirit to God, begging Him to "fix my wife" so we could have the marriage I knew He wanted for us.

Instead God showed me I was the one who needed to change, that the behavior of my wife, which I thought so in need of improvement was part of the "all things" that work together for my good according to Romans 8:28-29. God had a plan to conform me to the image of His Son, but that plan couldn't really begin until I humbled myself.

Today I am thrilled to say my wife and I are more in love with each other than at any other time in our marriage. It started with "God opposes the proud but gives grace to the humble."

Specific time spent with the Lord today and what was done:

_____

_____

Write out the memory verse for the week:

_____

_____

_____

_____

_____

_____

_____

_____

In your own words, write about what the Lord is saying to you through the Verses for today:

_____

_____

_____

_____

_____

How do the Theme for the Day and/or Week apply to your life now?

_____

_____

_____

_____

_____

_____

_____

As you were studying the word for today, what did you learn or discover?

_____

_____

_____

_____

_____

_____

Using the psalm you read today as a guide, write your own psalm to the Lord from your own heart:

_____

_____

_____

_____

_____

_____

_____

_____

_____

_____

_____

_____

_____

_____

Prayer requests and/or prayers answered (share with your Father from your heart):

_____

_____

_____

_____

_____

_____

What else is the Lord putting on your heart today?

_____

_____

_____

_____

_____

_____

_____

What other scriptures did you read today that were most impactful? How did they speak to you?

_____

_____

_____

_____

_____

Week #: **4**   Day #: **4**   Today's Date: _____

Chapter for the Week: **James 4**   Verses for today: **7-8**

Theme for the Week: **humility**

Theme for the Day: **draw near to God**

Word Study for Today: **submit**   Psalm for Today: **Psalm 73**

This is part of what I love about the book of James. We're getting into the meat here. You could spend weeks in just one of these verses, a year in the whole book of James. Of course that is true of pretty much any book of the Bible.

Which makes this a good moment to pause, and remind yourself that A Tithe of Time can be used again, with any book in the Bible. All scripture is God breathed. He can take any section of the Bible, and unfold it for you if you only give Him the time.

Here again in James, it comes down to time, quality time. Draw near to God and He will draw near to you. Hopefully you have been faithfully drawing near to God for the past three and a half weeks!

My wife and I have two daughters. There's lots of estrogen and not much testosterone, but God knew what He was doing. To spend time with my daughters one-on-one, I take my girls out individually on 'daddy dates'.

Sometimes it's longer in between our dates than I want it to be. All that either of them has to do is to come cuddling up to me asking for my attention and she pretty much gets it. If they draw near to me, then I will draw near to them. I can't help it.

How far beyond that level of love and desire for a relationship is our Heavenly Father? Both Matthew and Luke record the words of Jesus saying, "If you then, being evil, know how to give good gifts to your children, how much more will your Father which is in heaven give good things to them that ask Him?" Our Father is there, waiting for us to come to Him and ask Him for some time. Any moment you are willing to draw near to Him, He is there to draw near to you.

Specific time spent with the Lord today and what was done:

_____

_____

Write out the memory verse for the week:

_____

_____

_____

_____

_____

_____

_____

In your own words, write about what the Lord is saying to you through the Verses for today:

_____

_____

_____

_____

_____

How do the Theme for the Day and/or Week apply to your life now?

_____

_____

_____

_____

_____

_____

_____

_____

As you were studying the word for today, what did you learn or discover?

_____

_____

_____

_____

_____

_____

Using the psalm you read today as a guide, write your own psalm to the Lord from your own heart:

_____

_____

_____

_____

_____

_____

_____

_____

_____

_____

_____

_____

_____

Prayer requests and/or prayers answered (share with your Father from your heart):

_____

_____

_____

_____

_____

What else is the Lord putting on your heart today?

_____

_____

_____

_____

_____

_____

_____

What other scriptures did you read today that were most impactful? How did they speak to you?

_____

_____

_____

_____

_____

Week #: **4**   Day #: **5**   Today's Date: _____

Chapter for the Week: **James 4**   Verses for today: **9-10**

Theme for the Week: **humility**

Theme for the Day: **He will lift you up**

Word Study for Today: **humble**   Psalm for Today: **Psalm 10**

I have already shared that James 4:6 has been my theme verse for quite a few years. Directly connected to that verse is James 4:10. "Humble yourself in the sight of the Lord, and He shall lift you up."

This theme of humbleness is a reoccurring theme throughout scripture. As you study the word humble today, you will find it in the Bible over and over. It is used as a verb meaning anything from being "brought low" to being literally humiliated. It is also used as an adjective to describe a state of being.

Here in verse 10, it's a verb. God is saying if we will actively pursue the state of being humble, He will lift us up. This does not imply a single moment of humility, but the ongoing presence of humility in our spirit.

For years, my approach to life was something like this, "God gave me the talents and skills, now it's completely up to me to make something of them". While the first part of that statement was true, the second part was only partially true.

I do not believe God gives us talents, expecting us to sit still and do nothing until one day those talents blossom into full bloom and are a blessing to the entire body of Christ.

At the same time, it is not up to us to achieve the end. We cannot create the result God has intended. It is our responsibility to take action, to be about our "Father's business" to use the words of Jesus.

1 Corinthians 3:7 says "God gives the increase". We can do our part by using what God has given us for His glory. Be actively engaged in the process of choosing humbleness, but let God lift you up in His time.

Specific time spent with the Lord today and what was done:

_____

_____

Write out the memory verse for the week:

_____

_____

_____

_____

_____

_____

_____

_____

In your own words, write about what the Lord is saying to you through the Verses for today:

_____

_____

_____

_____

_____

How do the Theme for the Day and/or Week apply to your life now?

_____

_____

_____

_____

_____

_____

As you were studying the word for today, what did you learn or discover?

_____

_____

_____

_____

_____

_____

Using the psalm you read today as a guide, write your own psalm to the Lord from your own heart:

_____

_____

_____

_____

_____

_____

_____

_____

_____

_____

_____

_____

_____

Prayer requests and/or prayers answered (share with your Father from your heart):

_____

_____

_____

_____

_____

What else is the Lord putting on your heart today?

_____

_____

_____

_____

_____

_____

What other scriptures did you read today that were most impactful? How did they speak to you?

_____

_____

_____

_____

_____

Week #: **4**   Day #: **6**   Today's Date: _____

Chapter for the Week: **James 4**   Verses for today: **11-12**

Theme for the Week: **humility**   Theme for the Day: **slander**

Word Study for Today: **judge**   Psalm for Today: **Psalm 51**

Of all the sins we can commit against other brothers and sisters in Christ, perhaps slander is the most destructive.

Our flesh loves to hear a juicy story. That's why the entertainment world has made billions of dollars selling us stories about what is happening with people who are famous.

I have seen slander rear its head in a business setting, and I have personally been subjected to it. Within my company, over the years, I have had several Christian brothers who have blessed me with their words one moment, and were slandering me to others the next.

Even worse, I have seen this within ministries inside the church. When it happens there, it can be deadly, especially since it can be difficult to identify when it is happening.

It can come up when someone in authority over us does something we don't like. It can be we don't agree with a decision they made, sometimes it's the way we have been treated. However all authority is God ordained, so it's not our place to judge them, but to submit to them as to the Lord.

Guard your tongue against slander, don't even get close to the border of it. The Bible tells us to "flee all appearances of evil". So when you are about to "share" something with one person having to do with someone else, stop and ask yourself a few questions:
- Will the person I am speaking of be blessed by what I say?
- Will God be honored and glorified in all that I am about to say?
- Would I say this in the same way if that person also was here?
- Is this anyone's business but mine and the Lord's?

Specific time spent with the Lord today and what was done:

_____

_____

Write out the memory verse for the week:

_____

_____

_____

_____

_____

_____

_____

_____

In your own words, write about what the Lord is saying to you through the Verses for today:

_____

_____

_____

_____

_____

How do the Theme for the Day and/or Week apply to your life now?

_____

_____

_____

_____

_____

_____

_____

As you were studying the word for today, what did you learn or discover?

_____

_____

_____

_____

_____

_____

Using the psalm you read today as a guide, write your own psalm to the Lord from your own heart:

_____

_____

_____

_____

_____

_____

_____

_____

_____

_____

_____

_____

_____

Prayer requests and/or prayers answered (share with your Father from your heart):

_____

_____

_____

_____

_____

What else is the Lord putting on your heart today?

_____

_____

_____

_____

_____

_____

_____

What other scriptures did you read today that were most impactful? How did they speak to you?

_____

_____

_____

_____

_____

Week #: **4**   Day #: **7**   Today's Date: _____

Chapter for the Week: **James 4**   Verses for today: **13-17**

Theme for the Week: **humility**

Theme for the Day: **if the Lord wills**

Word Study for Today: **tomorrow**   Psalm for Today: **Psalm 90**

In Luke 12:13 Jesus relates the parable of the rich fool. God warns us not to hoard things for ourselves when we are not "rich toward God". The rich man assumed he would live long enough to enjoy his wealth. As a side note, this is the closest reference to someone trying to retire that you will find in the New Testament, and look at God's response. But that's a discussion for a different book.

We need to approach our lives with a sense of immediacy. We cannot presuppose God has ordained for us a certain number of days and we will have time to get around to the things He called us to do for His purposes.

Psalm 37:18 says "the Lord knows the days of the upright". Psalm 90:12 asks God to "teach us to number our days, that we may apply our hearts unto wisdom." Only God knows how long we will be on this earth.

Remember I'm a financial planner. All day, every day, I help people design long term financial strategies that to some extent presuppose on tomorrow. So I certainly can't say that I never plan for the future. And God is not saying planning for the future is wrong.

After all, God says in 1 Timothy 5:8 "if anyone does not provide for his own, and especially for those of his household, he has denied the faith and is worse than an unbeliever"! Ouch! Don't you have to plan for tomorrow in order to fulfill this obligation? So how do we reconcile this verse with our study in James?

The difference is in the area of hoarding, instead of being "rich toward God". Matthew 6:33 says we are to "seek first His kingdom and His righteousness, and all these things (the needs of this world) will be given to you". Focus on God's kingdom and let Him take care of this world.

Specific time spent with the Lord today and what was done:

_____

_____

Write out the memory verse for the week:

_____

_____

_____

_____

_____

_____

_____

In your own words, write about what the Lord is saying to you through the Verses for today:

_____

_____

_____

_____

_____

How do the Theme for the Day and/or Week apply to your life now?

_____

_____

_____

_____

_____

_____

_____

As you were studying the word for today, what did you learn or discover?

_____

_____

_____

_____

_____

_____

Using the psalm you read today as a guide, write your own psalm to the Lord from your own heart:

_____

_____

_____

_____

_____

_____

_____

_____

_____

_____

_____

_____

_____

_____

Prayer requests and/or prayers answered (share with your Father from your heart):

_____

_____

_____

_____

_____

What else is the Lord putting on your heart today?

_____

_____

_____

_____

_____

_____

What other scriptures did you read today that were most impactful?
How did they speak to you?

_____

_____

_____

_____

_____

Eight
A Tithe of Time, Week Five

Four weeks have gone by and less than two to go. You're hitting the top of the hill and will soon be accelerating down towards the finish. Stay focused on the Lord and continue practicing your time with Him daily.

If you stumble and get off track, just stand up, dust yourself off and keep going. God doesn't expect perfection, but he does examine our heart. Don't let the father of lies come in and try to rob you of the joy you are finding in your time with God.

As I have gone through the two and a half year process of writing this book, I find myself surprised (and yet not surprised) that the theme for our final week is perseverance.

Having made it almost all the way through this forty day process, we now need to persevere through the last week and a half. Don't give up or let go of your commitment.

Allow yourself to meditate on the Lord and His goodness. He is speaking to you and leading you down His path. Ask Him to continue to reveal to you what steps He has for you to take, and what great work He has for you to accomplish.

In some cases, in the Bible, the Lord revealed His entire plan to someone before they took action. Think of Gideon in the book of Judges. In other cases, God simply said "go" and expected that person to obey, just as He did with Philip in Acts 8.

I can't tell you exactly how God will speak to you, or how much He will say. It may be a word, it may be a whole story.

When God spoke to me several years ago about writing this book, the whole picture of the book, the format and even the structure using the book of James was all laid out in front of me. It was totally clear what God expected, and it was up to me to obey.

I will pray that God speaks to your heart and you obey what you hear. He has a plan for you and for your life. Through perseverance He will accomplish His will through you.

Week #: **5** Day #: **1** Today's Date: _____

Chapter for the Week: **James 5** Verses for today: **1-3**

Theme for the Day: **wealth**

Word Study for Today: **rich** Psalm for Today: **Psalm 49**

Memory verse for the week: **James 5:10-11**

The Bible can often seem like a massive contradiction in the area of wealth. On the one hand, so many of the great heroes of our faith were wealthy. On the other hand, we find repeated verses that seem to condemn those who accumulate wealth. Is wealth evil or wrong?

1 Timothy 6:10 is often quoted. "For the love of money is the root of all evil" (KJV). That seems to sum it up. However, let us notice clearly God is not saying money is evil. It is the love of money that is "a root of all sorts of evil" (NAS).

This is such a huge issue I have spent a great deal of time looking into this verse. First, I was interested to see which Greek word for "love" was used. What I found was that it's not a single word, but a phrase for "love of money". The root of that phrase, though I'm no Greek scholar, is also used in 2 Timothy 3:2 "men will be lovers of self, lovers of money, boastful…". It is also used in Luke 16:14 to describe the Pharisees.

When I looked up the word "all", I found it used elsewhere in the Bible not to mean literally 100%, but to imply a large percentage. Accordingly, I don't see God saying that all (as in every single instance of) evil comes from money, but that a large majority of evil grows out of the love of money.

You may want or need to spend more time in this verse than these few paragraphs. However I think we can summarize what James and much of the Bible are saying.

Money is the main thing on earth that has the potential to compete with God for our attention! God even singles it out, saying, "You cannot serve God and money." Your money, regardless of the amount, will either be a tool you use to serve God, or it will become your god. Beware!

Specific time spent with the Lord today and what was done:

_____

_____

Write out the memory verse for the week:

_____

_____

_____

_____

_____

_____

_____

_____

In your own words, write about what the Lord is saying to you through the Verses for today:

_____

_____

_____

_____

_____

How do the Theme for the Day and/or Week apply to your life now?

_____

_____

_____

_____

_____

As you were studying the word for today, what did you learn or discover?

_____

_____

_____

_____

_____

_____

Using the psalm you read today as a guide, write your own psalm to the Lord from your own heart:

_____

_____

_____

_____

_____

_____

_____

_____

_____

_____

Prayer requests and/or prayers answered (share with your Father from your heart):

_____

_____

_____

_____

_____

_____

What else is the Lord putting on your heart today?

_____

_____

_____

_____

_____

_____

What other scriptures did you read today that were most impactful? How did they speak to you?

_____

_____

_____

_____

_____

Week #: **5**   Day #: **2**   Today's Date: _____

Chapter for the Week: **James 5**   Verses for today: **4-6**

Theme for the Week: **persevere**

Theme for the Day: **pleasure and luxury**

Word Study for Today: **fattened**   Psalm for Today: **Psalm 112**

It seems like we've spent half our time in the book of James talking about the rich. If nothing else, this should be a warning to those who are, or desire to be rich.

We know that God longs to bless us. Those blessings can come in many forms, and often not in the way we expect. God is challenging us to think in eternal terms, not in the limited thinking of this world.

Wealth is a tool God can use for great good. It is also a tool the enemy can use for great evil. I have heard it said, "If you want to know a person's heart, look at their schedule and look at their checkbook." How true.

In this book, I've questioned how we spend the time God has given us. Since He created time, and gave us a limited amount, we should tithe of that time back to Him, just as we would tithe of our money. God established the tithe in part to help shift our focus off of what we have and on to the God who owns everything.

Look at your checkbook, and ask yourself how you are utilizing the resources God has placed in your hands. Ask yourself if you are a living example to the world as to how a Christian must be a steward. Examine your life and see if you are hoarding what you have instead of giving generously and spending your money fairly.

The Bible teaches us to pay people fairly, sacrifice ourselves when others are in need, and remember the things of this world are as "rubbish", Philippians 3:8, "compared to the surpassing greatness of knowing Christ Jesus". When the Lord audits your finances and asks you how you used them for His purpose, what will He find?

Specific time spent with the Lord today and what was done:

_____

_____

Write out the memory verse for the week:

_____

_____

_____

_____

_____

_____

_____

_____

In your own words, write about what the Lord is saying to you through the Verses for today:

_____

_____

_____

_____

How do the Theme for the Day and/or Week apply to your life now?

_____

_____

_____

_____

_____

_____

As you were studying the word for today, what did you learn or discover?

_____

_____

_____

_____

_____

Using the psalm you read today as a guide, write your own psalm to the Lord from your own heart:

_____

_____

_____

_____

_____

_____

_____

_____

_____

Prayer requests and/or prayers answered (share with your Father from your heart):

_____

_____

_____

_____

_____

_____

What else is the Lord putting on your heart today?

_____

_____

_____

_____

_____

_____

What other scriptures did you read today that were most impactful? How did they speak to you?

_____

_____

_____

_____

_____

Week #: **5**   Day #: **3**   Today's Date: _____

Chapter for the Week: **James 5**   Verses for today: **7-10**

Theme for the Week: **persevere**   Theme for the Day: **be patient**

Word Study for Today: **patience**   Psalm for Today: **Psalm 27**

"Lord give me patience and give it to me now!" Some variation of this statement has been around for ages. But in every humorous statement is a grain of truth. We are so impatient for everything, and in our fast paced world of instant gratification, we want everything now.

If we look at Biblical history, we find patience is to be prized, and God takes far longer than you or I might like to develop it. When the Lord called Abram out of Ur, he was seventy five. God promised to make him a great nation.

More than 10 years went by and Abram and Sarai still had no children. So Sarai went to Abram and convinced him to be with her servant, which was an accepted practice in ancient times. However, this was a demonstration that the patience God desired was not yet present. How often do we think we have to help God along? How much grief and suffering over thousands of years could have been avoided?

When Abram was ninety nine, the Lord reappeared to him and changed his name to Abraham. A year later, Isaac was born. Abraham had to wait 24 years until the Lord changed his name from Abram, and then only one year until the child of promise was born to him.

Think of Joseph in Egypt, or Moses spending forty years in Midian while the Lord refined him. In our lives, we think of a few years as a long time, and the concept of decades to wait for something is inconceivable. Yet to the Lord "a day is like a thousand years", 2 Peter 3:8.

Patience is a difficult trait to learn, but one God wishes to develop in us all. Ask the Lord to show you what great work He has for you, then patiently set about accomplishing the task He gives you.

Specific time spent with the Lord today and what was done:

_____

_____

Write out the memory verse for the week:

_____

_____

_____

_____

_____

_____

_____

In your own words, write about what the Lord is saying to you through the Verses for today:

_____

_____

_____

_____

How do the Theme for the Day and/or Week apply to your life now?

_____

_____

_____

_____

_____

_____

As you were studying the word for today, what did you learn or discover?

_____

_____

_____

_____

_____

Using the psalm you read today as a guide, write your own psalm to the Lord from your own heart:

_____

_____

_____

_____

_____

_____

_____

_____

_____

Prayer requests and/or prayers answered (share with your Father from your heart):

What else is the Lord putting on your heart today?

What other scriptures did you read today that were most impactful? How did they speak to you?

Week #: **5**   Day #: **4**   Today's Date: _____

Chapter for the Week: **James 5**   Verses for today: **11-12**

Theme for the Week: **persevere**

Theme for the Day: **the end intended**

Word Study for Today: **endure**   Psalm for Today: **Psalm 30**

Have you ever done business with a Christian, and after the transaction felt that you had been taken advantage of, overcharged or underserved? Why is it many people have a bad opinion of Christians as businesses or as consumers?

As Christians, we are called to a standard that is not of this world, but is far greater. It is not what we can get away with, but what God's standard is for us.

A few years back, I was friends with a Christian man who became disgruntled with some business partners. He worked with them for several years, signing multiple contracts governing his professional conduct.

When this Christian man decided to leave his partners, he broke every single contract he had made without apology, claiming the Holy Spirit gave him "peace about it". He attempted to justify his actions by saying "their contract isn't legally valid". Unfortunately he found out he was wrong legally and morally. His actions cost him not only a huge amount of money, but destroyed his witness for Christ.

As Christians we are to be held to a higher standard, as business owners employees or consumers. If you sign an agreement with someone, you are bound to keep your word, even if the world offers you a loophole. James is quoting Jesus Himself from Matthew 5:37, "let your 'yes' be 'yes' and your 'no,' 'no'; anything beyond this comes from the evil one."

We are called to be salt and light in the world. Our standard is that of God. In your business and personal dealings, ask yourself if your conduct would be the same if Jesus was the person you were dealing with.

Specific time spent with the Lord today and what was done:

_____

_____

Write out the memory verse for the week:

_____

_____

_____

_____

_____

_____

_____

_____

In your own words, write about what the Lord is saying to you through the Verses for today:

_____

_____

_____

_____

How do the Theme for the Day and/or Week apply to your life now?

_____

_____

_____

_____

_____

_____

As you were studying the word for today, what did you learn or discover?

_____

_____

_____

_____

_____

Using the psalm you read today as a guide, write your own psalm to the Lord from your own heart:

_____

_____

_____

_____

_____

_____

_____

_____

_____

_____

Prayer requests and/or prayers answered (share with your Father from your heart):

_____

_____

_____

_____

_____

_____

What else is the Lord putting on your heart today?

_____

_____

_____

_____

_____

_____

What other scriptures did you read today that were most impactful? How did they speak to you?

_____

_____

_____

_____

_____

Week #: **5**   Day #: **5**   Today's Date: _____

Chapter for the Week: **James 5**   Verses for today: **13-15**

Theme for the Week: **persevere**   Theme for the Day: **let him**

Word Study for Today: **forgiven**   Psalm for Today: **Psalm 72**

In our flesh, many of us think that we have to stand on our own. As men, we seem to expect that we can make it without any help. It has to get really hard before we'll ask for help.

In December of 2007, I started having gallbladder attacks. For anyone who has experienced this, you will have compassion for me. For those who haven't, it's worse than kidney stones and comparable (I've been told) to childbirth. The only good news is with a very strict diet of no meat (except fish) and no saturated fats, it can be somewhat controlled. But if I ate the wrong thing, the pain was terrible.

Between December and April of 2008, I had five attacks. All late at night between about midnight and two am. When this happened the pain was so intense I would literally throw up every 30 minutes for 6 to 8 hours.

In April, my ten year old daughter asked me why I hadn't gone up for prayer at church about the problem with my gallbladder. I had some Christian brothers and sisters who had prayed for me privately, but for whatever reason, the times when our church specifically invited people to come up for prayer in service, I wasn't experiencing any pain.

Here's a ten year old asking her father why he's not following the Biblical command to call on the elders to pray for him. I was floored, and had no good answer. Of course you can bet the very next Sunday I was up there receiving prayer. I did have my gallbladder removed about 8 months later as I kept losing weight, but the prayer lesson from my daughter remains.

James reminds us that we are not alone in this battle called life. The Lord is with us, and He has also given us fellow soldiers to fight the battle beside us. No man, or woman, is an island.

Specific time spent with the Lord today and what was done:

_____

_____

Write out the memory verse for the week:

_____

_____

_____

_____

_____

_____

_____

_____

In your own words, write about what the Lord is saying to you through the Verses for today:

_____

_____

_____

_____

How do the Theme for the Day and/or Week apply to your life now?

_____

_____

_____

_____

_____

_____

As you were studying the word for today, what did you learn or discover?

_____

_____

_____

_____

_____

Using the psalm you read today as a guide, write your own psalm to the Lord from your own heart:

_____

_____

_____

_____

_____

_____

_____

_____

_____

_____

Prayer requests and/or prayers answered (share with your Father from your heart):

_____

_____

_____

_____

_____

_____

What else is the Lord putting on your heart today?

_____

_____

_____

_____

_____

_____

What other scriptures did you read today that were most impactful? How did they speak to you?

_____

_____

_____

_____

_____

Week #: **5**   Day #: **6**   Today's Date: _____

Chapter for the Week: **James 5**   Verses for today: **16-18**

Theme for the Week: **persevere**

Theme for the Day: **effective fervent prayer**

Word Study for Today: **prayer**   Psalm for Today: **Psalm 17**

In the 1950s, Helen Roseveare was serving as a missionary in the Congo. She relates a story in her book *Living Faith* that has circulated on the internet as an email.

One night Helen found herself in charge of a two year old and a premature baby whose mother died as a result of childbirth. At night it was cold and drafty and Helen feared for the child's survival. Another woman was sent to stoke the fire and fill a hot water bottle but returned with the report that their last hot water bottle had burst.

The child survived the night, but would not survive for long without a way to stay warm at night. There was no possible source of a new hot water bottle. On most days, Helen visited the children in the orphanage and prayed with them. This day was no exception, and Helen shared about the premature baby and the dire circumstances.

One ten year old girl, Ruth, prayed to the Lord, "Please God, send us a water bottle. It'll be no good tomorrow, God, the baby'll be dead. So please send it this afternoon." While Helen was gasping inwardly at the audacity of the prayer, the girl added "and would you please send a dolly for the little girl so she'll know You really love her?"

Helen goes on to say that she felt put on the spot. How do you honestly say "amen" to that prayer? She says, "I just did not believe that God could do this." Yes, God can do anything, but there are limits, aren't there?

After all, the only way God could answer this particular prayer would be by sending a parcel from the homeland. At that time she had been in Africa for almost four years, and had never, ever received a parcel from home. And if someone did send a parcel, who would send a hot water bottle to a missionary who lived on the equator!

Helen goes on to share in her own words what followed: "Halfway through the afternoon, while I was teaching in the nurses' training school, a message was sent that there was a car at my front door. By the time that I reached home, the car had gone, but on the veranda, was a large twenty-two pound parcel. I felt tears pricking my eyes.

"I could not open the parcel alone, so I sent for the orphanage children. Together we pulled off the string, carefully undoing each knot. We folded the paper, taking care not to tear it unduly. Excitement was mounting.

"Some thirty or forty pairs of eyes were focused on the large cardboard box. From the top I lifted out brightly colored, knitted jerseys. Eyes sparkled as I gave them out. Then there were the knitted bandages for the leprosy patients and the children began to look a little bored. Next came a box of mixed raisins and sultanas – that would make a nice batch of buns for the weekend.

"As I put my hand in again, I felt the…could it really be? I grasped it and pulled it out. Yes, a brand new rubber, hot water bottle! I cried.

"I had not asked God to send it, I had not truly believed that He could. Ruth was in the front row of the children. She rushed forward crying out, 'If God has sent the bottle, He must have sent the dolly too!' Rummaging down to the bottom of the box she pulled out the small, beautifully dressed dolly. Her eyes shone. She had never doubted!

"Looking up at me, she asked, 'Can I go over with you, Mummy, and give this dolly to that little girl so she'll know that Jesus really loves her?'

"That parcel had been on the way for five whole months, packed up by my former Sunday School class whose leader had heard and obeyed God's prompting to send a hot water bottle, even to the equator. One of the girls had put in a dolly for an African child – five months earlier in answer to the believing prayer of a ten year old to bring it 'that afternoon'."

Pray that our faith would be as that of a child's. "The effective, fervent prayer of a righteous man (or child) avails much" (James 5:16).

Specific time spent with the Lord today and what was done:

_____

_____

Write out the memory verse for the week:

_____

_____

_____

_____

_____

_____

_____

_____

_____

In your own words, write about what the Lord is saying to you through the Verses for today:

_____

_____

_____

_____

_____

How do the Theme for the Day and/or Week apply to your life now?

_____

_____

_____

_____

_____

_____

As you were studying the word for today, what did you learn or discover?

_____

_____

_____

_____

_____

_____

Using the psalm you read today as a guide, write your own psalm to the Lord from your own heart:

_____

_____

_____

_____

_____

_____

_____

_____

_____

_____

Prayer requests and/or prayers answered (share with your Father from your heart):

_____

_____

_____

_____

_____

What else is the Lord putting on your heart today?

_____

_____

_____

_____

_____

What other scriptures did you read today that were most impactful? How did they speak to you?

_____

_____

_____

_____

_____

Week #: **5**   Day #: **7**   Today's Date: _____

Chapter for the Week: **James 5**   Verses for today: **19-20**

Theme for the Week: **persevere**   Theme for the Day: **save a soul**

Word Study for Today: **truth**   Psalm for Today: **Psalm 40**

Yesterday I shared with you a moving story of faith. I can't read the words of Helen Roseveare without being moved to tears. I find her story reminds me of God's faithfulness and convicts me as well. I expect that I, like Helen, would not have had the "audacity" to pray the prayer of faith the little ten-year-old girl prayed.

As we go through life, people let us down, opportunities pass us by, and in some cases it seems that God forgets to answer some of our prayers. We can't see His answers in the eternal, and in our limited view of life we think He's just not listening to us.

The book of James has challenged us to live out our faith daily. We are to choose joy even in our trials, let our works show the world our faith, practice peace, pursue humility, and learn patience.

"We know that all things work together for good to those who love God, to those who are the called according to His purpose" (Romans 8:28).

We know that verse, but most people cannot quote Romans 8:29, and never connect the two verses. "For whom He foreknew, He also predestined to be conformed to the image of His Son." It's great to know that God works all things for good for us. What is even more important is to know why He does. Romans 8:29 answers that question.

To conform us to the image of His Son, Jesus Christ. God has promised to use every moment in your life to help you grow into the image of Jesus. I pray that these past five weeks, and the next five days, will help you focus more on Him than ever before. In all that you do and learn, remember to ask God, "how are you using this for my good, to conform me to the image of your Son?"

Specific time spent with the Lord today and what was done:

_____

_____

Write out the memory verse for the week:

_____

_____

_____

_____

_____

_____

_____

_____

In your own words, write about what the Lord is saying to you through the Verses for today:

_____

_____

_____

_____

How do the Theme for the Day and/or Week apply to your life now?

_____

_____

_____

_____

_____

_____

As you were studying the word for today, what did you learn or discover?

_____

_____

_____

_____

_____

Using the psalm you read today as a guide, write your own psalm to the Lord from your own heart:

_____

_____

_____

_____

_____

_____

_____

_____

_____

Prayer requests and/or prayers answered (share with your Father from your heart):

_____

_____

_____

_____

_____

What else is the Lord putting on your heart today?

_____

_____

_____

_____

_____

_____

What other scriptures did you read today that were most impactful? How did they speak to you?

_____

_____

_____

_____

_____

Nine
A Tithe of Time, Week Six

When I was in high school, I used to run track. The mile was my favorite event, and I was pretty good. That run was a little over 4 laps around a standard size track. For the first three laps, I ran to keep up with the pack, and to make sure I was positioned well for the final lap.

Some runners knew they had to be well in front going into the last lap because they didn't have a strong kick at the end of the race. Others knew they had a strong kick and didn't want to be in front, just fairly close to the person in the lead so they could sprint past them at the very end.

A bell sounded as the final lap began. That is what it came down to, and the race would either be won or lost in that final lap. That sound you just heard was the bell going off for your final lap.

Over the past five weeks, you have spent more time with God than you probably have in the past five months, and possibly more than the past five years. You have drawn near to Him, and He has drawn near to you. In these final five days, you should be focusing on finishing this race well.

Reflect deeply on your experiences over each of the first five weeks. Look for the reoccurring themes God has been sharing with you, and to really get down to the intimate details of your time with the Lord.

Ask God to continue opening Himself to you as you give your heart and mind over to Him completely. All the time and effort you have invested in these recent weeks should come to fulfillment this week.

So there's the bell. The last lap has just begun. You've run the whole race well up till now, it's time to finish strong! This is where your opponent will try to rise up and prevent you from winning. Guard your time these next five days so that you can finish this forty-day race and win the prize! May God bless you this week as you reach the mountaintop!

Week #: **6**   Day #: **1**   Today's Date: _____

Chapter for the Day: **James 1**   Verses for today: **1-27**

Theme for the Day: **choice**   Psalm for Today: **Psalm 75**

The overriding theme for week one was *choice*. I believe almost everything in life is a choice. Choices can be as simple as what to wear, as profound as where we will spend eternity.

Some things in life we cannot choose. I cannot choose how others will behave, I cannot always choose the circumstances I find myself in, and I cannot choose the emotions I will experience. But I can choose my response to all these things.

When we face trials and challenges in our life, we can respond by complaining to God. Even without complaining we often find ourselves asking God to remove us from the difficult circumstances, or asking Him to fix the person causing us the problem.

Here's a soul searching question for you. Do you ever find that the same kind of problems or circumstances seem to come up in your life over and over? Could it be that instead of asking God to remove us from them, we should be asking God what it is He is attempting to communicate to us?

God is not surprised by your circumstances. He is not hearing your prayer and thinking 'I hope he can figure this one out because I didn't expect that to happen'! He is patiently waiting for us to 'get it', to ask Him, "Lord, what are you trying to communicate to me and how do You want me to grow in this situation?"

It does not matter where you have been, or where you are in life. What matters is your choice to daily take up your cross and follow Jesus, Luke 9:23. This is a choice we make day by day, minute by minute.

Challenge yourself to really fellowship with Him these last five days. Ask yourself the question as you review week one: What choices have I been making that need to change? What cross do I need to take up daily?

Review week 1. Summarize what God spoke to you about during the course of this week, and how He spoke to you through your time with Him. What did you learn or discover about yourself or the great work He has for you? Take a good amount of time to truly reflect on the first week and meditate on God's words to you. Ask Him to further speak to you and show you His desire for your life.

_____

_____

_____

_____

_____

_____

_____

_____

_____

How does the Theme for the Day apply to your life now?

_____

_____

_____

_____

_____

_____

_____

As you were studying the word for today, what did you learn or discover?

_____

_____

_____

_____

_____

_____

_____

Using the psalm you read today as a guide, write your own psalm to the Lord from your own heart:

_____

_____

_____

_____

_____

_____

_____

_____

_____

_____

_____

_____

Prayer requests and/or prayers answered (share with your Father from your heart):

_____

_____

_____

_____

_____

_____

What else is the Lord putting on your heart today?

_____

_____

_____

_____

_____

_____

What other scriptures did you read today that were most impactful? How did they speak to you?

_____

_____

_____

_____

_____

Week #: **6**   Day #: **2**   Today's Date: _____

Chapter for the Day: **James 2**   Verses for today: **1-26**

Theme for the Day: **faith/works**   Psalm for Today: **Psalm 77**

This second week should have been challenging for you. James 2 deals with the area of wealth, and not favoring those who are wealthy in the things of this world. The second half of the chapter deals with our works. We are not saved by our works, but if we truly have faith, then it should be expressed through those works.

In week one we talked about choice. The choices we make should affect the way we live our lives, and should be evidenced in the works we display and the fruit our lives bear.

In our actions on a daily basis, we are sharing Christ with the world. Those who are not saved will look at our lives, and to some extent will form their opinions of who Jesus is based on the works we have done.

Our works should set us apart. We have been called by Christ to serve. We have been bought with a price so dear to God as to be unimaginable. Who of us would willingly send one of our children to die for any cause? We would go in their stead if there was no choice, but to ask one of our children to lay down their life…I can't imagine.

Yet that is exactly what our Lord did. It goes beyond even our understanding because Jesus is not only the Son of God, but also and at the same time He is the Father. Jesus Himself said in John 10:30, "I and the Father are one".

If we truly believe these things, and have the faith in God we profess to have, then where is the fruit? How can we say Jesus is Lord, and then live as if the time we spend on earth is ours to do with as we wish?

Ask God to reveal to you where your works are not lining up with your faith. Let your faith guide you, and your works speak for you to an unbelieving world destined for hell.

Review week 2. Summarize what God spoke to you about during the course of this week, and how He spoke to you through your time with Him. What did you learn or discover about yourself or the great work He has for you? Take a good amount of time to truly reflect on the first week and meditate on God's words to you. Ask Him to further speak to you and show you His desire for your life.

_____

_____

_____

_____

_____

_____

_____

_____

_____

How does the Theme for the Day apply to your life now?

_____

_____

_____

_____

_____

_____

_____

As you were studying the word for today, what did you learn or discover?

_____

_____

_____

_____

_____

_____

Using the psalm you read today as a guide, write your own psalm to the Lord from your own heart:

_____

_____

_____

_____

_____

_____

_____

_____

_____

_____

_____

Prayer requests and/or prayers answered (share with your Father from your heart):

_____

_____

_____

_____

_____

What else is the Lord putting on your heart today?

_____

_____

_____

_____

_____

What other scriptures did you read today that were most impactful? How did they speak to you?

_____

_____

_____

_____

_____

Week #: **6**   Day #: **3**   Today's Date: _____

Chapter for the Day: **James 3**   Verses for today: **1-18**

Theme for the Day: **peace**   Psalm for Today: **Psalm 4**

James 3 is again a challenging section of scripture. As a Theme for the Week, I choose to reflect on peace. Peace is a choice we can make here on earth, and is also something that comes from God.

One scripture I love is Philippians 4:6-7. "Do not be anxious about anything, but in everything, by prayer and petition, with thanksgiving, present your requests to God. And the peace of God which transcends all understanding will guard your hearts and minds in Christ Jesus!"

Amazing. Just copying that scripture makes me want to take a week to dig into it. Every word is ripe with meaning and has volumes to say to us in our daily lives. What I take from it is a process.

"Do not be anxious" is a command. Quite literally this means dwelling in a state of anxiety is a sin. We can't control the fact that there will be moments when we become anxious. It's what we choose to do in those moments that determines if we are in sin or not.

God does not give us this command without telling us how to deal with it. When you become anxious, present your requests to God. He says to do so by way of prayer and petition, and specifically says to do this with thanksgiving! The thanksgiving part is difficult, but it is also the key.

It's easy to pray a prayer of complaint and petition God for what we need. In fact, I think too often that's what we do in our trials. However, we can be thankful God is not surprised by what we are going through.

Not only that, it is part of the "all things" mentioned in Romans 8:28 God uses for our good! Can you be thankful, even in the midst of your challenges, that God is aware of what is happening, and is actively working it out for your good? If you believe God is who He says He is, and the Bible is infallible, then you can truly experience peace at all times.

Review week 3. Summarize what God spoke to you about during the course of this week, and how He spoke to you through your time with Him. What did you learn or discover about yourself or the great work He has for you? Take a good amount of time to truly reflect on the first week and meditate on God's words to you. Ask Him to further speak to you and show you His desire for your life.

_____

_____

_____

_____

_____

_____

_____

_____

_____

How does the Theme for the Day apply to your life now?

_____

_____

_____

_____

_____

_____

_____

As you were studying the word for today, what did you learn or discover?

_____

_____

_____

_____

_____

_____

Using the psalm you read today as a guide, write your own psalm to the Lord from your own heart:

_____

_____

_____

_____

_____

_____

_____

_____

_____

_____

_____

Prayer requests and/or prayers answered (share with your Father from your heart):

What else is the Lord putting on your heart today?

What other scriptures did you read today that were most impactful? How did they speak to you?

Week #: **6**   Day #: **4**   Today's Date: _____

Chapter for the Day: **James 4**   Verses for today: **1-17**

Theme for the Day: **humility**   Psalm for Today: **Psalm 25**

In James 4, God hits us over the head with truth after truth. I think I could have taken this forty day study and spent the entire time in James 4! While there are many themes in this chapter, the overall theme I was drawn to is humility.

Every one of us struggles with pride. Falling into this sin leads to all sorts of related consequences. However, the Lord teaches us how to overcome pride, and that is by practicing humility.

Over the past three to four years, I have probably spent more time studying the word humble than any other word in the Bible. It's probably because I have struggled so much with pride God knows He can't just tell me once to be humble and leave it at that. He has continually been hammering my flesh with the concept of humility, and still does.

While I would love to say I've got it down (there's that whole pride thing again!) that would not be honest. I think it's like any addiction. "My name is William Jordan, and I'm addicted to pride." Thankfully God is patient with me, and picks me up when I stumble.

I want to encourage you as you review the fourth week, allow Him to search your heart for strongholds of pride. The Lord wants to use you for great things, but He wants, and should receive, all the glory. I need to give Him the glory for all things, this book being chief among them.

In my own flesh, there is no way this book could have been written. However, through this book He is showing you all you need is a willing heart and an ear to hear. Humble yourself before Him, and He will lift you up!

God has a great work for you to do. It's part of the reason you are here on this earth. Ask God to reveal any areas of pride or sinfulness that are hindering Him from doing the work He desires to do through you.

Review week 4. Summarize what God spoke to you about during the course of this week, and how He spoke to you through your time with Him. What did you learn or discover about yourself or the great work He has for you? Take a good amount of time to truly reflect on the first week and meditate on God's words to you. Ask Him to further speak to you and show you His desire for your life.

_____

_____

_____

_____

_____

_____

_____

_____

_____

_____

How does the Theme for the Day apply to your life now?

_____

_____

_____

_____

_____

_____

_____

_____

As you were studying the word for today, what did you learn or discover?

_____

_____

_____

_____

_____

_____

_____

Using the psalm you read today as a guide, write your own psalm to the Lord from your own heart:

_____

_____

_____

_____

_____

_____

_____

_____

_____

_____

_____

_____

Prayer requests and/or prayers answered (share with your Father from your heart):

_____

_____

_____

_____

_____

What else is the Lord putting on your heart today?

_____

_____

_____

_____

_____

_____

What other scriptures did you read today that were most impactful? How did they speak to you?

_____

_____

_____

_____

_____

Week #: **6**   Day #: **5**   Today's Date: _____

Chapter for the day: **James 5**   Verses for today: **1-20**

Theme for the Day: **persevere**   Psalm for Today: **Psalm 23**

I think it is only fitting our theme for day forty of this study is perseverance. If you have reached this day and have been faithful to give God a tithe of time for the last forty days, then you have persevered!

Reflect back on the day, not even two months ago, when you decided He was calling you to give Him a Tithe of Time. Think about how exhilarating and terrifying that prospect was. Your flesh undoubtedly rose up to oppose the idea, whereas your eternal essence knew how precious this time would be.

These past forty days have drawn you closer to God than you may have ever been before. It is right that we close this time with a reminder we are running a race that does not end with this forty day period of time.

God has called you to a life of significance. I truly mean that with all of my heart. My hope and desire is, through this period of time, you have begun to realize how greatly the Creator of the universe loves you, and how much He has that you can do for Him.

I can't tell you what God has for you. No one but the Lord knows your days and the steps that have been ordained for you. But I can share with you a story I heard from another pastor.

A man was called by God to go to a new area, minister to the people there and to raise up a church. God even showed him what the building was to look like. He was faithful, and God did what He said he would.

One day, this pastor found a man at the altar in the sanctuary weeping and crying. When he was able to speak, the weeping man told the pastor that years ago God had called him to come minister to these people, and to build a sanctuary on this spot, and even showed him what it would look like. The weeping man pulled from his pocket a rough sketch of the church they were now sitting in.

God's purpose will be accomplished. It is not because God needs you that you should persevere in following Him, but because God desires to bless you in great ways.

When I heard the story of that man, I realized God was speaking to me. I was going to be that man if I did not take action and persevere in the goal He had given to me. He gave me a great work to do, which was to write this book. It has taken me almost three years, but if I counted the actual time spent, it was probably less than a couple of months.

Had I not finally been faithful to what God was calling me to, He would still have accomplished His purpose. When I heard this story, I had a vision of myself walking through a bookstore and seeing a new book being featured. That book would be called *A Tithe of Time*, only there would be some other person's name under the title.

The thought drove me to action. God had called me to do something, and realizing I could fail so completely that the Lord would take the mantle He placed on me and give it to someone else was a terrifying thought. When God calls us to do something, we had better do it.

However the enemy does not want God's plan to be fulfilled. Our enemy will do anything he can to limit us in our effectiveness for God. I don't know about you, but Satan's favorite tactic against me is to distract me. It can be business or pleasure, but I will begin something and then lose my focus. To help us persevere, we need to be accountable.

For me, I went to my pastor, and to my small group. When I shared this book and my vision with my pastor, he got so excited. He turned around and preached my book right back at me with the passion and fire that I had when I began writing it. God gave him the words and the energy to pick me up and push me towards the finish. Thank you, Pastor Phil Munsey!

God has a great work for you to do! He is calling you to live a life that is significant, and leaves its effect on this and future generations. My prayer for you, at this moment, is that you will run the race not just to finish, but run in such a way that you will win the prize, 1 Corinthians 9:24.

Review week 5. Summarize what God spoke to you about during the course of this week, and how He spoke to you through your time with Him. What did you learn or discover about yourself or the great work He has for you? Take a good amount of time to truly reflect on the first week and meditate on God's words to you. Ask Him to further speak to you and show you His desire for your life.

_____

_____

_____

_____

_____

_____

_____

_____

_____

_____

How does the Theme for the Day apply to your life now?

_____

_____

_____

_____

_____

As you were studying the word for today, what did you learn or discover?

_____

_____

_____

_____

_____

_____

Using the psalm you read today as a guide, write your own psalm to the Lord from your own heart:

_____

_____

_____

_____

_____

_____

_____

_____

_____

_____

Prayer requests and/or prayers answered (share with your Father from your heart):

_____

_____

_____

_____

_____

_____

What else is the Lord putting on your heart today?

_____

_____

_____

_____

_____

_____

_____

What other scriptures did you read today that were most impactful?
How did they speak to you?

_____

_____

_____

_____

_____

Ten
Where Does God Want You to Go from Here?

Take a moment to think back to when you first picked up this book and thought, *I wonder if I can give God a tithe of my time and see Him do amazing things in my life?* Isn't it incredible to realize how much you've grown spiritually and how you've come to know the Lord on a deeper level?

If your experience has been like mine, and that of many others, you have been renewed and transformed by the Lord over these past 40 days. You have drawn nearer to God and He has drawn nearer to you. This has probably happened in ways that you never thought possible or haven't experienced since the early days of your faith.

In this chapter we will analyze the results of the time you have tithed to the Lord, and you will be encouraged to meditate on what you have heard from Him and discovered. Then you will take this knowledge and apply it to your plan moving forward. Finally, you will ask *and* answer the question, *Where does God want me to go from here?*

Read through the journaling summary and the questions from the final five days. Look and listen for prominent themes. Try to summarize what God has told you and revealed to you. What are your thoughts now?

1. What great work has God put on your heart to accomplish for Him?

_____

_____

_____

_____

2. What lifestyle change was the hardest for you to accomplish during the past 40 days? Why do you think it was difficult?

_____

_____

_____

_____

_____

3. What verses or book of the Bible did God repeatedly lead you to and why?

_____

_____

_____

_____

4. What did you learn about God in the last 40 days?

_____

_____

_____

5. What did you learn about yourself?

_____

_____

_____

6. What do you feel God is leading you to add or remove from your life?

_____

_____

_____

7. What else is on your heart right now?

_____

_____

_____

_____

8. Did you have an accountability partner following the 40-day Tithe of Time with you? If so, ask them what they have observed in your life during this time and record their words here.

_____

_____

_____

_____

9. Has anyone spontaneously shared with you changes they have seen in your life during the last 40 days? If so, record the comments and the name of the person who shared them here.

_____

_____

_____

_____

10. Who will you share these things with to help you stay accountable?

_____

_____

_____

_____

Now go back and retake the assessment from chapter one regarding your relationship with God and the fruit in your life. Score each question from 1 to 10, with 1 meaning "this is not true of me at all" and 10 meaning "this is extremely accurate concerning me."

• I feel close to God. _____

• God speaks to me and I hear His voice. _____

• My life is going the direction God wants it to. _____

• God is pleased with how I use my time. _____

• God has placed a great work in my heart that I am here to accomplish and I know what it is. _____

• God would say that I put Him first in my life. _____

• I am happy with the amount of time I spend with the Lord. _____

• Instead of leaning on my own understanding, I trust the Lord to direct my path. _____

• The fruit of the spirit (love, joy, peace, patience, kindness, goodness, self-control) is strongly present in my life. _____

• Others see Christ in me and comment on the differences in my life compared to when I wasn't a Christian. _____

Total up your score and write it here: _____

Copy your score from chapter one here: _____

Do you notice some differences? Summarize in your words the changes that have taken place within you, which are reflected in the answers you were able to give now, after your Tithe of Time.

_____

_____

_____

_____

_____

_____

Take a moment to go back and reread your answers to the questions in chapter two. What were your reasons for reading this book? What one thing did you want the Lord to do/change/speak to you about during this time? Note how the Lord has addressed those questions during the past 40 days.

_____

_____

_____

_____

_____

_____

Take time now to thank the Lord for all He has done for you. Note where you were spiritually 40 days ago and where you are now.

_____

_____

_____

Summarize the results. Write out a description of your successes and what you feel the most significant results have been. I encourage you to share them with your spouse or Tithe of Time buddy.

So Now What?

To quote the immortal words of Dr. Martin Luther King, Jr., you have "seen the mountaintop." God has opened Himself to you, and you to Him, in ways that you may not have experienced in years or decades, if ever. What happens now? As we have done throughout this book, let's turn to Scripture and revisit some of the references that point to the significance of the number 40.

Jesus went off alone into the wilderness for 40 days. At the end of this time, He was tempted. It's shocking to think that the Creator of the universe in the form of Jesus Christ could be tempted in any way. Yet in order for Jesus to truly be tempted, there must have been something in Him that would have wanted to and could have said "yes" to that temptation.

Now, if even Jesus was tempted, do you think that you might be?

In the Old Testament, Moses twice spent 40 days in the presence of the Lord receiving the Ten Commandments. Talk about a figurative *and* literal mountaintop! So what did Moses return to when he came down from the mountain? The whole nation had fallen into sin, and his own brother Aaron had formed an idol of gold for the people to worship.

Noah spent 40 days and nights in the ark listening to the rain. When the rain stopped, all wasn't well. He and his family spent approximately five months drifting on the water in the ark before it finally came to rest on the mountains. Even after the ark ran aground Noah was cooped up with all those animals for months before he was able to set foot on dry land.

The Israelites waited for 40 days for the spies to return from scouting out the Promised Land. When they returned, the whole nation failed in the first test of faith, which was to believe the good report that Joshua and Caleb gave about "the land flowing with milk and honey." Instead the people failed the test and didn't believe this report. They spent the next 40 years wandering in the wilderness while that faithless generation died off.

So what will happen to you?

Don't let down your guard. The enemy will want to attack you in an effort to weaken you after the spiritual growth you've experienced during the last 40 days. After great success comes the time when the enemy tries to damage or destroy what the Lord has built.

Think of Elijah calling fire down from heaven as recorded in 1 Kings 18:25. That's yet another great biblical example of a true mountaintop experience! But wait … what's the next thing he did? After receiving a message from the queen saying she would have his head, he turned tail, ran, and hid! Greater men and women than you and I have failed. Don't get lulled into a sense of complacency, but instead, remain on your guard.

Pray in faith for the breakthroughs that God has put on your heart. Most importantly, share this with strong Christian friends. Silence is your enemy. The Lord has planted seeds in your life during the past 40 days, but the "cares of this world" can come up and choke them off, halting any further growth. One of the best "weed killers" is the fellowship of other believers.

How do You Feel Now?

So do you feel closer to God? Do you feel more confident in hearing His voice and knowing His will? Here's an interesting question for you, one that isn't asked very often: In what ways did *God* change during the last 40 days? Write your answer here:

———————————————

That should have been an easy question. I even tipped you off by not giving you space to write more than the words "He didn't." God didn't change at all! So if your relationship with the Lord is vastly different, what changed? The challenging answer is that you did! That means that you, and you alone, have control over the relationship you have with God.

God is always ready to speak with us and to have a relationship with us. In Revelation 3:20 Jesus says, "Behold I stand at the door and knock. If anyone will open the door, I will come in and sup with him and he with me." While this scripture is often used as part of a call to salvation, the direct usage as recorded in the Bible was to those who were already saved!

The implication of this scripture is that some Christians have Jesus standing *outside* the door of their hearts. The God of the universe and your personal Savior is standing at the front door of your heart asking if He can come in and have dinner with you. Yet some of us leave Him standing outside while we carry on inside.

Are you ready for some good news? Jesus is continually standing at the door and knocking. This scripture is true today, it was true 40 days ago, and it will be true 40 years from now. At any time when a believer decides to hear His voice and open the door, Jesus will come in and spend intimate time with him or her!

The fundamental proof of this scripture can be found in the change in your life over the last 40 days. During that time you daily opened the door of your heart and invited Jesus in. You spent time with Him, every day talking with Him and listening to what He had to say. You invested in your relationship with Him and thus you have grown spiritual fruit as a result.

How many times have all of us been guilty of asking God when He was going to "show up" when He was standing there right beside us the whole time? God doesn't change.

Final Steps

Take a few hours to meet with your Tithe of Time buddy. Have them over for dinner, or if it's your spouse, get out of the house together for several hours. Share your experiences and what you heard from the Lord during the past 40 days. If you went through the Tithe of Time with a group, get everyone together for a special group meeting, or make this discussion the sole topic of your next regular weekly meeting.

Discuss the Following Questions:

What changes will you make in your life?

What time will you add back? What will you leave out permanently?

What are your plans, directions, and goals now?

Was this just an exercise in time management, or was this something that changed you on a deeper level?

I'm not suggesting that you keep the same schedule of time from now on, but maybe you've discovered that you don't want to go back to living exactly the way you did prior to beginning this study. Once God has stretched you, you should not resume your prior shape.

Maintain specific, purposeful time with the Lord daily. Seek His will in deciding how much time should be set aside. Do this first thing in the morning, if at all possible.

The Next 40 Days, the Next 40 Years ...

Here we are at the close of this experience. It is my sincere wish and desire that these past 40 days have been the life-transforming period that they were for me and for others who have read this book.

But here is the acid test: Where do you go from here? You see, these past 40 days could have been a nice break from the world, a sort of honeymoon with the Lord. Is the honeymoon over, or will you maintain the depth of relationship you have experienced during these past seven weeks?

In life, people truly do not truly stagnate. People are either growing or they are dying. There is no middle ground; there is either growth or decay, improvement or degeneration. To echo the words of the Lord through Joshua, "I have placed before you this day life and death ... choose life!" From this point going forward you have a choice as to the direction you will take. My challenge to you is to choose growth and life!

It is time to start a new 40-day plan. My encouragement to you is to live your life from now on in 40-day increments. Create a 40-day plan, live that plan, and then move on to a new plan. Not every 40-day plan will be as intense as this one. Just be intentional in what each 40-day plan will look like. In this way you can plan out the rest of your life, in 40-day increments, in Him.

As a part of your plan, you need to be in a regular small-group fellowship. You need to share your pain and your victory from this process with others who will keep you held up in prayer and who will hold you accountable to the work that God has prepared for you to do.

Each 40-day increment doesn't have to be as significant as the 40-

day Tithe of Time you've just accomplished. I would encourage you to go through this book again at least once a year to spend 40 days in a Tithe of Time mode.

It doesn't matter if you use the book of James as a guide, if you pick another book of the Bible, or if you do a word study on a new word daily. As long as you are in the Word and you use that as your foundational material, God WILL be there with you. It's His Word, after all!

Appendix
Time Sheets

Sample Time Sheet:

Time		Activity (15 minute segments - 8 hours)	Type
6:00	am	sleeping	S
6:15	am	read the Bible and pray	G
6:30	am	get up and shower	H
6:45	am	get ready	H
7:00	am	get ready	H
7:15	am	drive kids to school	M
7:30	am	drive kids to school	M
7:45	am	drive kids to school	M
8:00	am	drive to work	M
8:15	am	at work	W
8:30	am	at work	W
8:45	am	at work	W
9:00	am	at work	W
9:15	am	at work	W
9:30	am	at work	W
9:45	am	at work	W
10:00	am	at work	W
10:15	am	at work	W
10:30	am	at work	W
10:45	am	at work	W
11:00	am	at work	W
11:15	am	at work	W
11:30	am	at work	W
11:45	am	leave for lunch	M
12:00	pm	eat lunch	M
12:15	pm	eat lunch	M
12:30	pm	drive back to work	M
12:45	pm	at work	W
1:00	pm	at work	W
1:15	pm	at work	W
1:30	pm	at work	W
1:45	pm	at work	W

Key:

Type	Categories	Hours	%
G	God related	0.25	3%
R	Recreational	0.25	3%
W	Work related	4.75	59%
H	Household	0.75	9%
S	Sleeping	0.25	3%
M	Miscellaneous	1.75	22%

Blank Time Sheet:

Time	Activity (15 minute segments - 8 hours)	Type

Key:

Type	Categories	Hours	%
G	God-related		
R	Recreational		
W	Work-related		
H	Household		
S	Sleeping		
M	Miscellaneous		

ABOUT THE AUTHOR

William Jordan is a bestselling author of several books, including *Strategic Wealth*, and coauthor of *The Success Secret* with Jack Canfield of *Chicken Soup For the Soul* fame.

A nationally recognized expert in the fields of wealth management and financial planning, William has repeatedly been featured on CNBC and appeared as a repeat guest on *The Wall Street Journal Report with Maria Bartiromo*, seen on NBC, CNBC and CBS.

William has often been sought out for financial advice and has been quoted by *Forbes*, *Kiplinger's*, *The Wall Street Journal*, *Business Week* and *Time*, among many other nationally recognized publications.

A highly acclaimed public speaker, William has spoken on a variety of topics, both financial and spiritual in nature, to tens of thousands of individuals nationwide. William is also a member of Mensa, the international high IQ society, and enjoys reading, singing, and exercising in his spare time.

William and his wife Tiphanie have been happily married since 1995 and are busy raising their two daughters, Savannah and Skye. Having filled several key areas of lay leadership within his local church, William places a high value on biblical wisdom and the inerrancy of scripture and is currently pursuing his Masters of Divinity through Trinity College of the Bible and Theological Seminary.

www.ingramcontent.com/pod-product-compliance
Lightning Source LLC
Chambersburg PA
CBHW070953040426
42443CB00007B/482